Pushkin's
The Queen of Spades

Neil Cornwell

Bristol Classical Press
Critical Studies in Russian Literature

First published in 1993 by
Bristol Classical Press
an imprint of
Gerald Duckworth & Co. Ltd
61 Frith Street
London W1D 3JL
e-mail: inquiries@duckworth-publishers.co.uk
Website: www.ducknet.co.uk

Second edition 2001

A catalogue record for this book is available
from the British Library

ISBN 1-85399-342-5

Printed in Great Britain by
Antony Rowe Ltd, Eastbourne

Contents

Preface to Second Edition

For the second edition of this study, the main text remains unaltered. I have, however, taken the opportunity of adding a 'Postscript' (in the form of three brief notes) to the Appendix on the Count Saint-Germain. I have also been able to provide an addendum updating the Bibliography with a number of the items to have appeared since 1993. One article listed then as 'forthcoming', that by S. Dalton-Brown, has now at last been published (in *Russian Literature*, 46, 2000, 289-98). The connection between *The Queen of Spades* and James' novella *The Aspern Papers* has attracted further attention (see in particular Joseph S. O'Leary, 'Anathemata for Henry James', *English Literature and Language*, 36, 1999, 63-99) and remains an ongoing offshoot of comparativist interest. In addition, the Pushkin bicentennial activities of 1999 are still giving rise to collections of published papers. It scarcely needs saying that, in the new millennium, scholarship on *The Queen of Spades* continues on its merry way.

N.C.
(Bristol, 2001)

Acknowledgements

Permission is gratefully acknowledged to the following for allowing me to include reprinted illustrative material: James Forsyth (and Bristol Classical Press), for his diagram of Hermann's three card games; Nathan Rosen (and the editors of *Slavic and East European Journal*), for pictures of period Russian playing cards; and Michael Pursglove (and the editors of *Irish Slavonic Studies*) for his chronological table. I am also grateful to Tony Briggs, for reading and commenting on my typescript.

Introduction

'You don't mean to say that there are Russian novels?...', the Countess says to her nephew in *The Queen of Spades*. There were Russian novels in 1833, but not written by Pushkin. The nearest Pushkin was to come to a novel was *The Captain's Daughter* (1836), published only weeks before his shockingly premature death in a duel. This was a historical romance set in the era of Catherine the Great and the Pugachev rebellion, written somewhat in the manner of Sir Walter Scott but with the Pushkinian advantage of concision. Pushkin's other completed 'novel' was *Eugene Onegin* (1823-30), written in verse. And yet Pushkin, as he turned his attentions ever more to prose from the later 1820s, did aspire to the novel form; accounts of his progress through prose and his novelistic attempts, ranging from the regrettably unfinished to the no more than fragmentary, have been chronicled by Paul Debreczeny (1983) and David Budgen (1990) and indeed translated (in anthologies of Pushkin's prose fiction compiled by Debreczeny and Gillon Aitken – see Bibliography). Pushkin's main achievements in prose though are slightly more modest in scale. He boasts the story cycle *The Tales of Belkin* (1830), five near-contemporary short stories, framed by an elaborate narrative and 'editorial' device; and the tale *The Queen of Spades* which, judged by its continued popularity, its influence, the adaptations to which it has given rise (theatrical, operatic and cinematic) and common critical consensus, has to be regarded as Pushkin's masterpiece in prose.

The Queen of Spades was written during Pushkin's famously productive 'Boldino autumn' of 1833 and published in 1834 (first in the journal *Library for Reading* and later the same year in a book-collection of Pushkin's tales); the manuscript of the final version seems not to have survived. It was an immediate popular success, initially largely for reasons of plot: gamblers were keen to try Hermann's 'three, seven, ace' system for themselves. Later its style was to attract equal attention. Its merits and its appeal were quite self-evidently such that serious criticism of the story scarcely seemed necessary in the nineteenth century, though a number of obvious markers were established (predictably enough by Belinsky but more notably by Dostoevsky).

As this study will show, it is the twentieth century which has taken up *The Queen of Spades* and subjected it to seemingly endless analysis. This really took place for the first time during the Formalist period of Russian criticism and went on up until the War. Again this process restarted, this time in the

West, and largely in Anglo-American criticism, in the 1960s. Russian criticism, however, continued to play its part and Part One of this study (and the Bibliography) will demonstrate both the extraordinary quantity of criticism which has been generated by this tale of modest length and the variety of readings which have been produced. This state of affairs, and the on-going popularity of *The Queen of Spades* as a student text (not to mention its ever growing familiarity to the general reader through a plurality of translations), made it a natural choice as one of the opening titles of this newly launched critical series.

Part One of this study will survey the critical literature on *The Queen of Spades*, concentrating to a large extent on twentieth-century views. While it is not claimed that the criticism consulted is completely comprehensive, a large cross-section, at the very least, has been examined. Part Two aims to present something in the nature of a textual commentary, to synthesise and develop previous readings and to suggest lines along which the acceptability or otherwise of a plurality of readings may be judged.

To reduce the number of notes, references (from the Bibliography) have been incorporated into the text, with page numbers (e.g. 'Debreczeny, 1983: 100'); as the year given will be taken from the edition used, rather than year of first publication, the reader is asked to bear with occasional apparent infelicities (e.g. 'Pushkin: 1948'). The transliteration system used here is that of The Library of Congress (minus diacritics), with the exception of surnames ending in 'y' (such as 'Dostoevsky' or 'Tolstoy') and the soft sign at the end (here omitted, e.g. 'Gogol'), other than in the Bibliography (where 'ii' or 'oi' endings etc. are used) or where other usage is in quotation. Translations are my own unless otherwise stated.

Part One

Faîtes vos jeux!

The Queen of Spades has been called many things, from an 'anecdote' (by Belinsky: see below) to an extremely compressed novel (A.V. Chicherin; see Debreczeny, 1983: 232). While seen by Abram Lezhnev in 1937 as 'avoiding contrived plot construction' (Lezhnev, 1983: 141), it actually displays a considerable discrepancy between *fabula* (logical 'fable', or basic storyline) and *siuzhet* (plot presentation within the text: see Shukman, 1977; Pursglove, 1985). Nevertheless, in a naive sense at least, the plot does appear to bear an almost classical simplicity; and yet Lezhnev (1983: 126) felt equally able to term it 'this most complicated of Pushkin's stories, so difficult to understand'. Anna Akhmatova too has remarked: 'How complicated *The Queen of Spades* is! Layer upon layer' (Chukovskaia, 1976: 21).

The Queen of Spades is certainly compressed. It is some twenty-five pages in length (thirty in the Penguin edition of Rosemary Edmonds' English translation) and it gives rise to a number of what are by now commonplaces in Pushkin criticism generally: its condensed form and precision of style are seen as almost poetic in nature; the verbal texture is seen as full of subsidiary meaning and potentially portentous connotation; scarcely a word is held to be superfluous; and even some of the rhythms of poetry have been discerned in Pushkin's prose. Such factors must be what has led to the astonishing body of criticism devoted to this single short work of fiction: in particular the proliferation of interest in this text during the first half of the twentieth century, and the veritable explosion in the second half.

Before going any further with the critical history of this complex and apparently contradictory tale, it might be advisable – *pace* Prince D.S. Mirsky, who declared 'the story cannot be summarized' (Mirsky, 1958: 119) – to set out a brief synopsis.

The tale opens (Chapter I) in the 'present' (about 1830) during a card session in the St Petersburg rooms of a Horse Guards officer named Narumov. Among the guests is a young officer of Engineers, Hermann, who is of German origin and who never gambles himself but observes the play keenly. Tomsky, another member of the company, remarks that his octogenarian grandmother, the Countess Anna Fedotovna, also does not play – despite the circumstances of an anecdote, which he then proceeds to narrate:

3

Sixty years before (i.e. about 1770) she was the rage of Paris, known there as *la Vénus moscovite*. Having lost a considerable sum at cards to the Duke of Orleans, which her husband refused to cover, she faced financial and social ruin. In desperation, she turned to the Count Saint-Germain, an occultist of dubious repute. Saint-Germain gave her a three-card tip, with the aid of which she retrieved her loss against the Duke. Thereafter the Countess revealed the formula to no one except, some years later, a young man named Chaplitsky, who also won with it, having promised never to play again, and has since died in poverty.

In Chapter II, Tomsky discusses the possibility of introducing Narumov to his grandmother; the latter's young ward, Lizaveta Ivanovna, is disappointed that Narumov is not an engineer, as a young officer of that calling has been watching the house and attempting to pay court to her. The engineer in question is Hermann, who, having become obsessed by the secret of the three cards, finds himself drawn, as if by 'a mysterious force', to the house of the Countess; having briefly considered the feasibility of gaining the secret by becoming the lover of the 87-year-old Countess, he has spotted Lizaveta Ivanovna and decides she might be a better bet to gain access to the house. Following the receipt of a flurry of *billets doux*, Lizaveta Ivanovna (Chapter III) agrees to a nocturnal assignation with Hermann, instructing him to enter the house and await her return with the Countess, from a ball. This Hermann does, but waits in the Countess' study, rather than going up to Lizaveta's room. After the return of the ladies, Hermann emerges to confront the lone Countess and demand the secret. Getting no reply other than 'It was a joke', Hermann loses control, calls the Countess an 'old witch' and threatens her with a pistol, whereupon she expires. Hermann then goes up to Lizaveta Ivanovna to confess all. Lizaveta is distraught and calls Hermann a 'monster'; nevertheless she gives him a key to enable him to leave the house unseen (Chapter IV). More from superstition than remorse, Hermann goes to the funeral service for the Countess (Chapter V). When he approaches the coffin, he thinks he sees the dead woman wink 'mockingly' at him. Having wined and dined himself, contrary to his normal custom, in his confusion Hermann returns home to sleep it off, waking at a quarter to three in the morning, when he seems to receive a visitation from an old woman, whom he recognises as the Countess. This visitor tells him that he may win by playing the three, seven and ace, in that order, at the rate of one card a day, and never again in his life; he will earn her forgiveness if he marries Lizaveta Ivanovna. The three, seven and ace, we are told in the climactic Chapter VI, become an *idée fixe* in Hermann's mind, crowding out the image of the dead Countess. He thinks of gaming in Paris, but is brought by Narumov to the gambling salon of Chekalinsky, newly arrived from Moscow. There Hermann wins on the first night with a three and on the second night with a seven, but on the third, as he thinks he holds the winning ace, his card turns out instead to be the queen of spades, whose image on the card appears to wink at him, uncannily resembling 'the old woman!' A short 'Conclusion' reports that Hermann has gone out of his mind, Lizaveta Ivanovna has married the prosperous son of the former steward of the Countess and is bringing up a poor female relation, and Tomsky is marrying his society princess.

The Queen of Spades on its publication in 1834 was greeted with high praise by its readers, largely for its striking plot. Journal reviews were on the whole more reserved, although at least one critic, Osip Senkovsky (editor of *Library for Reading*), greeted Pushkin's stylistic achievement as a model for Russian prose; P.V. Annenkov commented that the general success of 'this light and fantastic story' is explicable by the presence of characters from contemporary society: one should look elsewhere for deep, poetic design in Pushkin (see, among others, Sidiakov, 1960: 206; Poliakova, 1974: 374; Lerner, 1929: 136). The relationship of Pushkin's tale (whether parodic or serious) to European romantic and Gothic literature (in particular to certain tales by Hoffmann and to French freneticism, both being fads sweeping Russia at the time) scarcely needed stating by critics in that period. Such antecedents, parallels and possible sources were subsequently 'rediscovered' in abundance by twentieth-century commentators. *The Queen of Spades* could also be readily accommodated within the burgeoning form of the 'society tale', which was soon to be absorbed as one of the staple ingredients of the nineteenth-century Russian 'realist' novel. Even in modern times (i.e. the 1950s), Anna Akhmatova considered that 'no one wrote a more courtly-society piece, ever' (Akhmatova, 1986: 404 n.8). Most importantly, its entertainment value was supreme; elucidation seemed almost superfluous.

Soon after first publication, Pushkin noted in his diary: 'My "Queen of Spades" is in great vogue. Gamblers are betting on the trey, the seven and the ace' (Debreczeny, 1983: 188-9). The first adaptation, a stage version by the then popular dramatist A.A. Shakovskoy entitled *Chrysomania, or the Passion for Money*, followed as early as 1836 (and has been described as 'an absurd and tasteless reworking' – Alekseev, 1984: 113). An operatic version (*La dame de pique*), with a libretto by Scribe and score by Halévy, was performed in 1850. The story was still as popular in 1890, when Tchaikovsky's operatic *The Queen of Spades* was first staged.[1]

The mainstream of nineteenth-century Russian literary criticism, with its radical and utilitarian bias, although concerned to place Pushkin (as national bard) within its delineation of a progressively developing Russian literature, was less than seriously preoccupied with romantic or Gothic prose, especially of the popular or apparently self-explanatory sort. Belinsky, for instance, a brief ironic notice and then passing references apart in his voluminous articles on Pushkin, seems to have devoted just one short paragraph reassessing *The Queen of Spades*, although his praise of it is no doubt sincere. He wrote in *Notes of the Fatherland* in 1846:

'The Queen of Spades' is not a proper novelette [*povest'*], but a masterly short story [*rasskaz*]. In it are sketched surprisingly truly the old Countess, her ward, their relationship and the strong, but demonic and egoistic character of Hermann. It is not a proper novelette, then, but an anecdote [*anekdot*]: for a novelette, the content of 'The Queen of Spades' is too exceptional [or 'exclusive', *iskliuchitel'no*] and fortuitous [*sluchaino*]. But as a short story – we repeat – it represents the height of mastery. (Belinsky, 1953: 577)

Belinsky, then, along with many, appreciated Pushkin's artistry in *The Queen of Spades*, but must have been less enthusiastic about its surface occultism (or even its reliance on 'fortuity') and its high-society ethos (or 'exclusivity'). Altogether, it lacked for him the qualities of 'typicality' [*tipichnost'*] and national spirit [*narodnost'*] which he sought in literature, being imbued instead with the 'exceptionality' of the aristocratic 'anecdote', on which no doubt he knew the tale to have been at least partly based. Nevertheless, as we shall see, the points he made were to be repeated or expanded throughout later criticism.

The origins of *The Queen of Spades* have been variously traced, then, to Pushkin's own earlier abandoned prose fragments (see Debreczeny, 1983: 189-94); to an actual society anecdote involving the then still living (and aged 92) Princess Golitsyna who had allegedly, many years before in Paris, received the advice of Saint-Germain and subsequently therewith enabled her grandson to regain a loss by playing a certain three cards (and other variants on a similar story, see ibid.: 201-2); and to a supposedly autobiographical episode of an amorous nature (ibid.: 202-4). As we shall see, hidden meanings derived from Freemasonry have since been discerned, along with various literary derivations and an influence of the folkloric-fairy tale tradition. John Bayley has summed up some of these sources at least in the following neat formulation (Bayley, 1971: 323):

Thus the story grew up from abandoned story-projects and the characters in them, was grafted on to an anecdote from real life, and given a colouring of fashionably literary *diablerie*.

Chernyshevsky thought *The Queen of Spades* excellently written but of no great importance, a view shared by Saltykov-Shchedrin (Sidiakov, 1960: 206). Tolstoy, though, enthused about *The Queen of Spades* as Pushkin's *chef d'oeuvre* (ibid.: 215) and it had received wide acclaim in Europe through translation.[2] However, it was Dostoevsky (who had of course made his own use of elements from Pushkin's story in both *Crime and Punishment* and *The Gambler*), in remarks made in a letter of 1880, who provided a vital pointer for future critics:

> ...the fantastic in art has its limits and its rules. The fantastic must be so close to the real that you *almost* have to believe in it [Dostoevsky's emphasis]. Pushkin, who gave us almost all artistic forms, wrote 'The Queen of Spades' – the epitome of the art of the fantastic. You believe that Hermann really had a vision, exactly in accordance with his view of the world, and yet, at the end of the tale, that is when you have read it through, you cannot make up your mind: did this vision emanate from Hermann's nature or was he really one of those who are in contact with another world, one of evil spirits hostile to man. (N.B. Spiritualism and the study thereof.) That's art for you! (Dostoevsky, 1988: 192)

Dostoevsky's intuitive hesitation between the 'reality' or otherwise of Hermann's vision (within the terms of the fiction) – or in other words between a psychological and a supernatural interpretation of the story – was to become a cornerstone of more recent theory of the literary fantastic and *The Queen of Spades* to be seen as a prime example of the genre.[3] We shall return later to a consideration of this type of reading.

Les jeux sont faits!

Most criticism of the first two decades of the twentieth century, like that of the nineteenth, felt able to pass its judgements, and to make or refute interpretations, without seeing any necessity to justify its pontifications by careful analysis or by close reference to the text. Nevertheless, even by such cavalier critical methods, interesting views can occasionally emerge.

Vladislav Khodasevich (who was subsequently to become a leading émigré poet and a highly accomplished critic) in an early piece dated 1914 (published 1915 and again in 1922) considered *The Queen of Spades* as a Pushkin 'Petersburg story', along with *The Little House in Kolomna* and *The Bronze Horseman*, in which 'dark powers' engaged with representatives of mankind. In the case of *The Queen of Spades*, however, the initiatives came from man (Hermann; or indeed initially woman, the Countess in her Paris days) rather than from the powers themselves. Hermann indeed is seen as another 'little' man, rather than a superman, but one determined to rise socially, by means of even the supernatural: therein lies his rebellion ('*bunt*', Khodasevich, 1971: 89). Khodasevich notes a reversal in the plot, following the Countess' death: Hermann, instead of being the aggressor he has been up to that time, becomes virtually a victim instead, as the Countess' ghost is the one to impose upon him. The result of her machinations is that Hermann goes out of his mind, as do the protagonists of the other two works (Pavel and Evgenii) grouped by Khodasevich.

Mikhail Gershenzon (in 1919), taking up Belinsky, wondered why Pushkin should have produced 'such a strange, highly improbable anecdote' – or rather was it just 'the prank of a pen of genius' (Gershenzon, 1983: 97)? The storyline, in his view and in terms of the supposed relation of a series of facts, amounts to an 'utter absurdity'. Gershenzon seizes on Tomsky's anecdote (the anecdote within an anecdote, except that for Gershenzon *The Queen of Spades* 'is not an anecdote at all', ibid.: 98). Apart from anything else, Tomsky's anecdote is too good, too well told, to be from Tomsky at all (this is seen by Gershenzon as an artistic flaw in itself, as is Pushkin's depiction of details of the Countess' bedroom beyond 'what Hermann could and must notice at that minute of highest tension': p. 111). The initial reactions of the listeners to Tomsky's anecdote are in some part correct: 'Hermann's soul is set alight by an empty, clearly invented fairy tale, related by a frivolous officer as his guests are due to leave' (*skazka*, 99). The three cards envisioned as named as the result of Hermann's 'passion' are themselves therefore a mere fortuity (*sluchainost'*: 102). How then does Hermann seem to succeed in winning? Again it is seen as a matter of chance: fortune favours the brave (twice in Hermann's case) and then deserts him, or leads him to blunder in his manic delusion. The story thus seems to emerge as a satirical society tale again, rather than an anecdote of true artistic design; although its appeal has not diminished, it remains, in comparison to subsequent literary developments, 'not a picture, but a pen-sketch' (111).

The 1920s, however, brought the advent of the Formalist school of criticism and this left its mark, as on much else, on assessments of *The Queen of Spades*. In a brief but seminal essay first published in 1923, A.L. Slonimsky took up Dostoevsky's point from 1880 (though quoting only Arkadii's view from *A Raw Youth* that Hermann is a 'colossal figure' and the 'type of the Petersburg period') of hesitation until the very end on the reader's part. Slonimsky isolates three fantastic moments in the tale: Tomsky's anecdote, Hermann's vision and Hermann's win. He points out, in relation to the last named (which he sees as the only genuinely fantastic point) that the ace does in fact win (though not for Hermann!). 'As the tale goes on', writes Slonimsky, 'the fantastic element is instilled more and more deeply into the course of events and achieves its triumph at the end' (Slonimsky, 1963: 520); the mere 'anecdote' of Chapter I is transformed into 'reality' in Chapter VI, as the story moves 'from "anecdote" to "marvel" ' (ibid.).

Slonimsky draws attention to the three replies elicited by Tomsky's anecdote: '*sluchai!*', '*skazka!*' and '*poroshkovye karty?*' ('chance!', 'fairy tale!' and 'powdered cards?', to which we shall have more than one occasion to return later). He was also the first to notice Hermann's own prefiguring within the text of the three-seven-ace formula, the rhythmic character of the prose at certain key points and the dual (fantastic and realistic-psychological) motivation throughout, undercut by hidden realistic hints and Pushkin's spirit of irony (foreshadowed in the epigraphs). In a collision between the 'contemporary' world and the 'old', Hermann is seen as more in tune with the 'old world' Countess than with the 'contemporary' Lizaveta Ivanovna; with Hermann thus drawn to the past, 'the detailed description of old-world furniture harmonises perfectly with Hermann's withdrawal into the fantastic' (ibid.: 524-5, contrasting with Gershenzon's view). Hermann's 'fiery imagination' and the game of dual motivation makes a simple 'anecdote' into 'a masterpiece of narrative art': 'everyday life [*byt*] and the fantastic merge...into a single harmonious whole' (525).

Slonimsky has here provided an astonishingly acute critical skeleton which future commentators, whether aware of their debt to him or not, will expend considerable energy in fleshing out. One is almost tempted to suggest that Slonimsky had said everything that really needed to be said in 1923;

however, there is no such thing as the last word and, elaboration of Slonimsky's analysis apart, new approaches still remained to be essayed.

If Slonimsky had noted rhythm within Pushkin's prose in *The Queen of Spades*, in particular the incantatory quality of *tróika, semërka i tuz* and variations thereupon (522), the leading Formalist versification theorist, Boris Tomashevsky, used the tale as an exemplary text in a detailed philological study of rhythm in Russian prose. Tomashevsky's initial count of sentence length in the first two chapters of *The Queen of Spades* led to 'variegated figures' (Tomashevsky, 1929: 263). In addition to the length of sentences, Tomashevsky considered syllables, stress and intonation (at the beginning and the end of sentences, as well as within them), providing a series of statistical tables and diagrams to illustrate his findings. Unfortunately, his conclusions do not seem to have been particularly illuminating. 'It is not possible to talk of "verse quality" or "bumps" in prose independently of the results of collating prose fragments with metric patterns', he writes (ibid.: 285); and finally that poetic rhythmic patterns are perceptible within the texture of prose only through 'some external device (anaphora, structural repetitions etc.)' (317). While the poetic nature of Pushkin's prose in *The Queen of Spades* may be widely felt, even rigorous analysis seems to be unable to pin it down in meaningful quantifiable or qualitative terms, as has been pointed out much more recently (see William Edward Brown, 1986: 224).

'*The Queen of Spades* is nervously compact like a compressed spring', wrote D.S. Mirsky in 1926, in what appears to have been the first book in English on Pushkin; furthermore, Mirsky's appreciation of the attraction of this tale 'to the modern mind' now seems prophetic in view of the later plethora of critical attention (Mirsky, 1974: 183). Unfortunately Mirsky has little enough space himself for much beyond plot summary (notwithstanding his denial in his *History of Russian Literature* of the feasibility of such an exercise in the given case) and quotation, though he does refer to the tale's 'cold and concentrated glamour...tempered by a no less cold and essentially "classical" irony' (ibid.: 186).

A further leading Formalist, Viktor Shklovsky, writing in 1937, was at that time (in his *Notes on Pushkin's Prose*), able to be less openly methodological than he might have been a decade or so earlier; nevertheless, his remarks on *The Queen of Spades* remain not without interest. Shklovsky describes the Countess' appearance before Hermann as 'reduced realistic mysticism', contrasting it with the practice of Ann Radcliffe who, although her supernatural happenings always turned out to be 'explained', did not surround them at the time of their appearance with realistic details or hints.[4] According to Shklovsky, too, 'ghosts of the 30s liked to complete their unfinished earthly business' (Shklovsky, 1937: 65). The ghost of the Countess, however, in Shklovsky's view, 'deceives Hermann, laying down conditions and then not fulfilling its promise' (ibid.); this curious view is based on Hermann's purported ultimate intention of not abandoning Lizaveta: an unusual reading, though perhaps not an impossible one. Although Shklovsky at first appears to accept a supernatural interpretation, he nevertheless declares that he wishes 'to establish the absence of mystical content in the tale', thus apparently trying to have it both ways. At the end, as the mysticism disappears, he avers, as in Pushkin's 'The Coffinmaker' (from *The Tales of Belkin*): 'the win of two cards in a row is fantastic, but the [ensuing] loss is realistic' (ibid.). Shklovsky then proceeds to stress parallels between Hermann and Julien Sorel (of *The Red and the Black*), but sees Pushkin as in 'conflict' with Stendhal (70).

Abram Lezhnev [pronounced 'Lezhnyóv'], a moderate and sophisticated Marxist critic who was shortly to disappear in Stalin's purges, also published a book on Pushkin's prose in 1937. Although running to some two hundred pages, it has no sustained analysis of *The Queen of Spades* but refers intermittently to various aspects of the work: speech (Lezhnev, 1980: 92-3); an attempted refutation (rather pointless – perhaps included for political reasons: 98-103) of Slonimsky's somewhat Formalist views on rhythm; and other matters. Elements of comparativism and watered-down Formalism mingle with a basic Marxist aesthetic, as stylistic elements of Pushkin's prose are closely compared with examples drawn from his contemporaries and his predecessors, as well as consideration being paid to Russian successors and European counterparts.

The idea of a 'multiplicity of interpretations' appears to be countenanced, along with the wry comment as to 'how many pens have been blunted proving the correctness of one or the other explanation!' (ibid.: 125). The importance of irony is again stressed; the presence of secrets, triples and a fairy tale analogy are also noted. What Lezhnev sees as 'the obvious psychological paradox' is said to be 'revealed with the invincible correctness of a mathematical proof' (139). *The Queen of Spades* indeed is termed by Lezhnev 'a psychological story without psychology'; 'In Pushkin motivation is revealed through action. In Tolstoi or Dostoevsky', in contrast, 'the action itself is revealed in the motivation' (149); this is followed later by an interesting discussion of Hermann and Raskolnikov (167-8). All the more surprising then, in view of such insights, is Lezhnev's contention as to the 'simplicity' of *The Queen of Spades*, in that 'it unwinds events in their linear sequence, avoiding contrived plot construction' (141). Lezhnev admits only one case of 'a rearrangement of events in the story' (140). Such a position now seems difficult to sustain in the light of more recent detailed articles, which, as we shall see, lay bare the actual chronology of the tale, in terms of the discrepancy between *fabula* and *siuzhet*.

Viktor Vinogradov, another leading Formalist critic and a specialist in stylistics, published two major essays on *The Queen of Spades* (in 1936 and

1941). In the first of these he concentrated heavily on the details of the card game (faro) and the terminology surrounding it; other examples in the background literature of the time of the phenomenon of 'three true cards' and such like manifestations (drawing also on the work done by D. Iakubovich: 1933 and 1935; N.O. Lerner: 1929, who had undertaken considerable research into the historical background, and others); and the (particularly contemporary) symbolic potential of cards and card games. Vinogradov then goes on to examine, for the first time in any real detail, the narrative method employed by Pushkin in this tale, noting the varied narratorial poses as (apparent) participant (Chapter I), observer (Chapter II) and subsequently historian and even (virtually) 'cine-technician' (Vinogradov, 1980: 208). He also proceeds to observe the quirks in narrative time (in contrast to the more naive view taken in this respect by Lezhnev) and switches in point of view. Vinogradov is able to demonstrate that the composition of the tale allows the reader limited access to the inner world of Hermann and of Lizaveta Ivanovna, by means often of an interweaving of external narrative and internal perspective, but not to that of the Countess. Particular attention is also paid to the function of dialogue and exclamations. Vinogradov then proceeds to conduct a more technical linguistic discussion of the relationship between syntax and semantics, direct and indirect speech and the formation of syntagma and sentence.[5] Finally in this essay, Vinogradov discusses Pushkin's lexicon.

In the second essay, from his book *Pushkin's Style* of 1941, Vinogradov begins to build further on Slonimsky's remarks of 1923 by discussing the relationship in *The Queen of Spades* between the 'past' and the 'present', stressing the importance of the events and the ethos of 'sixty years ago' and concentrating on parallelisms between Chekalinsky and the Countess, Chekalinsky and Chaplitsky, and the card games of Chaplitsky and Hermann. Pushkin has succeeded, in Vinogradov's view, in bringing out two sides of 'artistic reality': the romantic mystery of the past and the 'new' qualities, such as that of calculating selfishness, of 'today': i.e. 1830 (Vinogradov, 1980: 259). Gershenzon is deemed to be 'of course wrong' about Hermann and the past (ibid.: 261 n.7). Concepts of ambiguity, symbolism and mask, as well as parallelism, are seen to be employed. This is particularly the case in respect of Hermann's vision of 'the white woman' (267), which leads on to his total mania over the three cards, resulting finally in 'the old woman' squeezing out the ace (268). Vinogradov concludes what is, perhaps inevitably for the period, ultimately a psychological reading (though with plenty of attention paid to double meanings and ironies) with a close examination of the presentation of Lizaveta Ivanovna (including parallels between her and the Countess) and of Hermann (linking him with the concept of 'fairy tale': 279). Hermann's monologue to the Countess is analysed and he is seen ultimately as 'the fanatic of a single dream' (281).

Thus what was essentially the Formalist period of critical analysis of *The Queen of Spades* (which had seen, for the first time, sophisticated attempts at a rigorous close reading of the text) was concluded. Virtually all the most likely approaches had now been at least broached, with the exception of a Freudian version of the psychological reading (which was not really possible in Stalin's Soviet Union). Much of the groundwork was therefore now in place for the somewhat baroque elaborations which were to follow in the post-war and post-Thaw period to come.

Rien ne va plus?

Soviet criticism, like Soviet literature, was in the doldrums during the last years of Stalin. After his death in 1953, the Thaw period began at least partially to revive literary life, including scholarship on the Romantic period, on Dostoevsky and on other frowned-upon areas. This process began to make itself felt in the late 1950s and through the 1960s, when new editions of the less obviously formalistic work of the Formalists (e.g. Slonimsky) also began to reappear.

One of the fruits of this improved scholarly milieu was the creation of the series *Pushkin: researches and materials*, which was launched in 1956. In the first volume of this series, M.P. Alekseev published a long and detailed article entitled 'Pushkin and the science of his time', part of which dealt with *The Queen of Spades*, in respect of the 'pseudo-sciences' mentioned therein of Galvani and Mesmer[6] and of Hermann's attitude to such matters as an 'engineer' (including details of Pushkin's familiarity with the background to engineering studies of the time). Alekseev also took issue with Gershenzon's criticism of the depiction of the details of the Countess' aristocratic dwelling, all of which he claims serve to confirm the apparent authenticity of Tomsky's anecdote; indeed, he affirms, there is 'not one unnecessary detail, not one superfluous word' in this description (Alekseeev, 1984: 116).

G.A. Gukovsky, another of the better Marxist critics who was allowed to publish from time to time, provided a firm psychological reading of *The Queen of Spades* in his book on *Pushkin and Problems of Realist Style*. Gukovsky concentrates mainly on the figure of Hermann, 'the process of the penetration of capitalism into the very basics of Russian life' and 'the depiction of the black power of money' (Gukovsky, 1957: 341). Hermann is seen as 'raising a revolt against the upper-crust world' in the name of bourgeois individualism (ibid.: 345). So far this is just another vulgar sociological reading, but Gukovsky's qualities as a critic are, at times, apparent. He talks of the ' "montage" of scenes from two epochs' (349) and draws a distinction between eighteenth- and nineteenth-century attitudes to the ethos of card games. He deems the final win of the 'three true cards' (given that the ace also wins) the only conceivably fantastic event (and evidence that the Countess did not 'deceive' Hermann, contrary to some readings: 365) but nevertheless appears content to put this down to 'chance' or 'fate'. Returning to things material, Gukovsky ascribes what he calls the 'colouring of the fantastic' to the style of the time, an epoch dominated ultimately by 'the soulless and senseless power of money' (366), in which 'gaming' stands as 'the quintessence of the stock-exchange and speculation' (367).

L.V. Chkhaidze returned to the card game, providing another precise summary of its rules, also in order to contest Slonimsky's contention that the fantastic is maintained until the end. Wishing to discredit any form of 'mystical' interpretation, he stresses the psychological elements. He does this in particular by developing Slonimsky's observation that at least the 'three' and 'seven' of the wining formula are prefigured in Hermann's musings; not only is this so, but Chkhaidze demonstrates that these multiples, in the event of three wins in each of which the original stake plus winnings so far are staked each time, are inbuilt into the course of a game played in this manner (and therefore do not need Slonimsky's hint of cabalistic significance):

1st day   2nd day   3rd day
47 + 47 = 94   + 94 = 188   + 188 = 376 (Chkhaidze, 1960: 458)

The tripling of the original stake (47,000 roubles) would give 141,000 (plus the stake of 47, equalling 188,000) after the second successful game; a sevenfold gain (of 329,000 which, with the original stake of 47 makes the final total of 376,000) would be the result of the successful completion of game three, on the third day in this case (according to the rules laid down by the Countess). Pushkin's notebooks had shown similar calculations (ibid.). Chkhaidze is also ready with an explanation as to how Hermann could inattentively 'draw the wrong card' (*obdërnut'sia*), owing to cards in a new pack sticking together:

> A strong but impressionable man, who had long observed the games of others and who well knew how it was possible to win, and how much, inspired himself [with auto-suggestion] as to which cards, arising from the game, to place his stake on, but at the last moment an unforseeable carelessness caused him to lose, to the complete collapse of all his desires. (ibid.: 459)

So far so good, but many commentators, of course, have not been so easily convinced that Hermann could simply thus 'inspire' his wins, not to mention other details of the story which may still require some explaining.

L.S. Sidiakov, also writing in 1960 (in an essay placing Pushkin's prose within the development of the novella in Russia in the first half of the 1830s), supplies a useful run-down of reactions to *The Queen of Spades* in its own time and thereafter, concentrating largely on the work as a society tale;

however, in so doing he goes over much ground that has already been covered, adds little or nothing new, and strangely omits any mention of the fundamental contributions made by Slonimsky and Vinogradov.

The early 1960s was a period when a new generation of post-war-trained anglophone Slavists began to make its mark upon Russian literary studies. It was not long before attention began to fall upon *The Queen of Spades* and, once it did, things soon began to snowball.

The first article of the Anglo-American new wave was published in 1962 by Joseph T. Shaw and, apparently well-versed in Russian criticism of the Formalist period, he approached *The Queen of Spades* through its epilogue (or rather 'Conclusion', as it is termed by Pushkin). 'Details given in [Pushkin's] epilogs', writes Shaw (1962: 115), 'may be assumed to be not "superfluous", but information that could not be known from the story proper and which is necessary for understanding it'. Firstly, Shaw notes that the epilogue contains three very short paragraphs, dealing with the fate of three characters: Hermann, Lizaveta Ivanovna and Tomsky. 'Parallelism in reverse' is seen in the fates of Hermann and Lizaveta Ivanovna (in the manner already observed by Vinogradov), while 'Germann is shown to have failed completely; Lizaveta Ivanovna and Tomsky are presented as having succeeded in their hopes' (ibid.: 116), in a progression suggesting 'failure, tainted success and success' (117).

Shaw's article is a fascinating mixture of insight and speculation. He notes the little-recognised importance of Tomsky (by virtue of his very presence in the epilogue) and sees the 'ace' (*tuz*) prefigured in the story (along with the 'three' and the 'seven') by Hermann's ambition to become an 'ace' (the word having the same double meaning in Russian as in English); he further sees the double possibility of Hermann's winning and losing reflected in the text (119), notes the levels of meaning of *schast'e* (happiness, chance and fate: 120) and explores the implications of the terms 'ace' and 'lady' (*tuz* and *dama*) for Lizaveta Ivanovna and Tomsky, as well as for Hermann. He is already, however, ready to re-launch the dubious procedure of assuming (or deducing) information from beyond the text by surmising, for instance, Lizaveta Ivanovna's husband to be a German (like Hermann: 121). Nevertheless, he also identifies Hermann's actual three crimes (as opposed to those loosely imputed to him by Tomsky): his deceiving of Lizaveta Ivanovna, his responsibility for the death of the Countess, and his loss of his patrimony (123 n.18). He further applies the concepts of calculation and imagination to the epilogue's three characters. Certain speculative touches apart, Shaw's article is a worthy successor to the labours of Vinogradov.

In 1963 the British student text series (calling itself 'The Library of Russian Classics' and published by Bradda Books) produced a Russian text of *The Queen of Spades* with apparatus in English, edited by James Forsyth (reprinted subsequently as a Blackwell Russian Text and most recently by Bristol Classical Press, from which edition quotes are now made). Forsyth contributes a lively introduction and linguistic plus background notes which both display and facilitate a keen reading of the text. He revives Dostoevsky's view of the tale and balances the supernatural and realistic interpretations; particulary useful though is his account of the game 'faro' (or *pharaon*, also known as *shtoss* or *bank*), presented clearly for the first time in English (Forsyth, 1992: 35-6); and even more useful is his diagram of 'Hermann's Three Games' (ibid.: 62).[7] This diagram (see Fig. 1) shows in the clearest possible manner the three games, Hermann's cards actually played, the banker's cards played and, graphically displayed down the left, or 'sinister' side (in Russia, 'the left has been unlucky from at least the thirteenth century' – Ryan and Wigzell, 1992: 662), the 'three true cards' as named by the Countess but bungled by Hermann: the cards which actually won the three games.

Charles Passage, in his book *The Russian Hoffmannists*, examined Hoffmannesque elements in *The Queen of Spades*, concluding that 'no single [Hoffmann] story can be adduced as a direct source' (Passage, 1963: 138), although there are motifs present which could derive from a number of the German's tales (including 'Gamblers' Luck' and 'The Sandman', as well as the novel *The Devil's Elixirs*): ultimately, 'the story is all Puškin's' (ibid.).[8] At the same time, Passage himself contributes to a psychological interpretation of the story by stressing the view that it essentially represents the progressive stages of 'the struggle between a mind and an idea'; the mind is finally 'reduced to a single thought fixed permanently on the exacerbated nerve of consciousness: "Trey seven, ace! Trey, seven, Queen!" ' (132-3). As for the supernatural, 'Romantic motifs are either spoofed or made to serve as symbols for a realistic purpose' (131), while, as far as Tomsky's anecdote is concerned, 'the whole episode is a delicious *canard*' (132).

Harry Weber introduced the legends and ceremonies of Freemasonry into discussions of *The Queen of Spades*, seeking to see in Pushkin's tale 'a new treatment of the Masonic legend of the murder of Hyram-Abif, the chief architect of Solomon's Temple' (Weber, 1968: 435). Furthermore, he argues (ibid.: 440), 'the entire scene between Germann and the old Countess is a parody of the Masonic initiation rite for the degrees of Apprentice and Master'. Weber bases his case on Pushkin's own Masonic connections; on near-coincidences in the names of Masons and those of Chaplitsky and Chekalinsky; on the fact of Hermann ending his days in the Obukhovskaia hospital (the director of which had been a prominent Mason); plus an accumulation of details of setting, gesture, speech and numerology. In addition to these revelations, Weber notes, more obviously and more prosaicly, that the tale consists of seven parts (six chapters and the short 'Conclusion') and contains three main characters; in the epilogue, he considers

HERMANN'S THREE GAMES

HERMANN'S CARDS

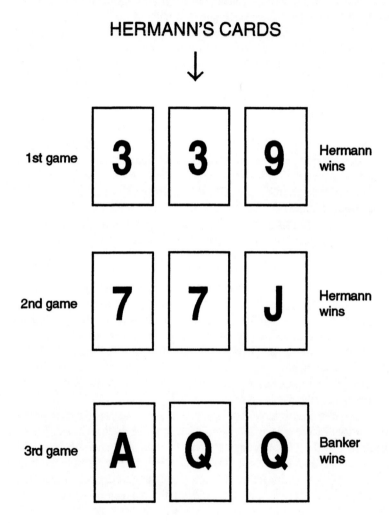

Fig. 1 Hermann's Three Games (reproduced by permission of James Forsyth).

Tomsky to have replaced the departed Countess ('his presence is necessary chiefly numerically': 443).

At the end of the 1960s, F. de Labriolle (in an article in French) once again put the case for a psychological interpretation, listing the six known 'facts' of the story 'which seem incontestable' (Labriolle, 1969: 262-3). All of these are seen as having a realistic explanation, although this is often arrived at by going outside the text or, at best, elaborating on possible hints from the text (assuming the Countess to have been the mistress of either Count Saint-Germain or the Duke of Orleans and subsequently of 'the young Chaplitsky', and the 'secret' of the cards a cover for the paying-off of debts by means of amorous intrigue, ibid.: 265).[9] Even were we to accept these arguments (and we shall return to such possibilities again later), Labriolle offers no explanation at all (not even those already encountered of 'chance' or 'inspiration') for the sixth incontestable fact of the story, that Hermann wins the first two games against Chekalinsky by following his acquired or imagined system.

Also in 1969, the Soviet comparativist N.Ia. Berkovsky made notes for an article on *The Queen of Spades* which were only published nearly two decades later (see Virolainen, 1987). Berkovsky stressed links between Pushkin and Dostoevsky, seeing Lizaveta Ivanovna (the sister of the old moneylender in *Crime and Punishment*) as an extension, as well as namesake, of Pushkin's poor ward. Hermann he sees in strong moral terms, with his principal crime 'desire for the three cards' (ibid.: 65): an absolute and secret weapon for the exclusive and personal control of chance and a bid for 'naked privilege and monopoly' (66). Material power is seen as an embourgeoising 'idol' (*kumir*) in *The Queen of Spades* and Pushkin's critique of 'absolutism' as lying behind the Napoleonic allusions in the depiction of Hermann.

Another commentator to concentrate on the development of Pushkin's prose in subsequent Russian literature in a wide-ranging fashion was Iu. Seleznev, who dealt in particular with *The Queen of Spades* as a basis for *Crime and Punishment*. However, Seleznev also has useful comments to make on Pushkin *en passant*, concerning both genre and time, as well as a readiness to admit the supernatural. *The Queen of Spades*, as well as three of the stories from *The Tales of Belkin* belong, in Seleznev's view, to the genre of the 'novella', as opposed to the more leisurely tale ('novelette' or short novel), in that the former consists of 'a strange event with an unexpected ending' and thus lends itself perfectly to Pushkin's compressed style, as well as pointing forward to the plot-twists of Lermontov and Dostoevsky (Seleznev, 1974: 421).[10] Seleznev also deals with 'psychological' time in the story, the 'unexpectedness' at each turn of events and the theme of madness.

In a valuable article of 1977, O.S. Murav'eva surveys much of the Russian criticism of preceding years, including a number of items not considered here (reminding us of the highways and byways into which Russian criticism extends and the practical difficulties involved in serious pretensions to comprehensivity), as well as Polish articles and a couple of American ones (Gregg, 1966; Weber, 1968). Among the items which Murav'eva discusses are important contributions by Iurii Lotman and by S.G. Bocharov, to which we shall return later. Her general thrust is to point to unresolved arguments over the fantastic, which have exercised so many commentators, and to stress that a 'realistic' reading based on chance is to admit a 'chain of chances and improbable coincidences [which is] nevertheless fantastic' (Murav'eva, 1977: 221). Some commentators have opined that this would be more fantastic than the supernatural itself(!). Critics who strive to uncover a 'key' to unlock the 'real' (and usually in the end realistic) meaning of *The Queen of Spades* are sagely deemed to reduce the tale to a simplistic reading: even Lotman's parameters are seen as 'too narrow' (225) to deal with the unfathomability and mystery of Pushkin's work. The remainder of the article deals with the dangers of approaching Pushkin's texts through the artistic systems of later writers, such as Dostoevsky. One critic always seen to be on sound ground, however, is Vinogradov.

In her follow-up article on the fantastic, a year later, Murav'eva expands on some of the issues she has already raised, stressing that attempts 'to remove from discussion the question of the fantastic' in scholarship on *The Queen of Spades* (as Gukovsky, 1957 had claimed to wish to do) were doomed to failure (Murav'eva, 1978: 62). She argues (as had Poliakova, 1974) that the fantastic permeates the texture of the work – not only the three cards and the apparitions, but the characters as well – to a point of 'incessant hesitation', as 'double meaning and dubiety extend even to the undeniably real images and events' (ibid.: 69). Once again, we shall be returning to fantastic readings.

The critical surveys conducted in such studies as that by Murav'eva (1977) are then a timely reminder of the formidable task involved in aiming at anything like all-inclusive coverage of criticism of *The Queen of Spades*. Indeed, one might well question the necessity for this: Victor Terras, in his recent *A History of Russian Literature*, considers that Pushkin's story in any case 'has been overinterpreted' (Terras, 1991: 241). Regardless of whether this opinion is to be accepted (and, even if it were, the fascinating question still remains as to why this should have been so), space and time, given the further explosion of commentary on the work through the 1970s and 80s, dictate that critical works should henceforth be grouped, according to the approach taken, and/or that only studies raising new points or readings should be accorded attention. Such a policy will be operated, though with some flexibility, from now on.

A number of articles on *The Queen of Spades* have been concerned with locating the sources of the plot of that story within earlier texts. Some of these have revived suggestions concerning Balzac and Stendhal, French freneticism, Hoffmann and Goethe's *Faust*. Others have picked on new or more specific models, such as Clas Livijn's *Spader Dame* (1824), which may have been known to Pushkin through Fouqué's German translation, *Pique-Dame* (1826), or a yet-to-be-traced French version; or the novels of Jules Janin (in particular *Barnave*, 1831).[11] As usual, none of these provides a satisfactory parallel to Pushkin's tale, although possible or even probable minor traces from each can be seen in *The Queen of Spades*. The whole question of genre, model and influence will lead us back subsequently to parodic readings.

Several Russian commentators in the 1980s have attempted to look more closely at the historical background to *The Queen of Spades* (following on the work of N.O. Lerner, 1929 and others). On the basis of what is known of the movements of actual historical figures – the Countess' supposed proto- type (Princess Natalia Petrovna Golitsyna, née Chernysheva, 1741-1837), the mysterious Comte de Saint-Germain (on whom, more anon) and more minor figures in the supposed drama (Richelieu, le Duc d'Orléans and Zorich) – it is argued that the 'sixty years ago' really refers to the 1760s rather than the normally supposed 1770s: the only time in which the necessary players were actually in Paris together was probably 1761 (although the young Natalia Chernysheva was then not yet married to Golitsyn; see Vilenchik, 1985). In any case, Golitsyna herself was never known as *la Vénus moscovite* (on the contrary, she was later dubbed 'Princesse Moustache'); the former appellation was in fact associated with her elder daughter, Ekaterina Vladimirovna (a renowned beauty, later the Countess Apraksina: Lerner, 1929: 149). An article published three years later in a further issue of the same organ (*Periodical of the Pushkin Commission*, Mil'china, 1988), going over much the same ground but preferring to concentrate on Golit- syna's sojourn in Paris of the 1780s, seems to contradict the thrust of Vilenchik's argument while studiously omitting any mention thereof. A third piece (Esipov, 1989) takes on board Vilenchik's main premise and develops it into new historical territory.

The supposed dating of the first card game to 1761 or 1762, the Countess' connection with Saint-Germain and Saint-Germain's known presence in St Petersburg in 1762 (and his alleged involvement in the events which deposed Peter III and put Catherine on the throne) are seen to establish a subtext of subversion. The second game between Chaplitsky and Zorich is likely to have taken place near the end of the eighteenth century (Zorich died in 1799), a time close, it is argued, to the assassination of Paul in 1801. What bigger 'game of chance' can there be than 'the struggle for the throne' (Esipov, 1989: 197 and 205)? Such a perceived subtext is heightened by the choice of epigraph to Chapter I ('And on nasty days/ they gathered/ often' etc.), known to be a Pushkinian imitation of Bestuzhev and Ryleev's agitational songs of the pre-Decembrist days (plus the guards officer milieu with its 'serious business'). The fact of Pushkin's having written these verses (and possibly first conceived the tale) as early as 1828-9, and the first fragmentary draft of what was to become the tale, beginning 'Four years ago we gathered, a number of young people, in Petersburg...' (ibid.: 200), suggest even that the 'true' date of the setting of *The Queen of Spades* could be 1825. A second 'n' was added to Hermann's name ['Germann' in Russian]; a dictionary of Russian names is said to point up the significance of this as follows: 'German – one's own [or native], pureblooded – a Latin name; Germann – a warrior, bodyguard – an old teutonic name' (203). In addition, it is claimed that the Decembrist leader Pavel Pestel 'was of German origin' and that Pushkin had sketched Pestel with a Napoleonic profile (ibid.).[12]

Fascinating as all these details may be, a sustained reinterpretation of the story based on such data is not supplied. One may yet emerge, and it would presumably welcome the ammunition provided by Lauren Leighton's essay on gematria in *The Queen of Spades* and discovery therein of the cryptonym 'Kondratii F. Ryleev' and other Decembrist allusions (Leighton, 1977B, a work of American scholarship seemingly not known or accessible to Esipov, even in the heady days of *glasnost'*). The argument would presumably be that in *The Queen of Spades* Pushkin was encoding messages of support for the Decembrist movement and critical of the house of Romanov; this has already been argued as the real purpose behind *The Tales of Belkin* by Andrej Kodjak.[13] The possibility of a politico-historical reading extending to a historical-mythic one is hinted at by Joanna Hubbs, who sees the Countess as both the Empress Catherine and Baba Yaga (Hubbs, 1988: 218), especially if we bear in mind both the events of 1762 (in which Saint-Germain and maybe even the young 'Countess' or her prototype may have had some part) and a detail supplied by Lerner back in 1929 (and seemingly not picked up since) that Golitsyna (née Chernysheva) may have been a granddaughter of Peter the Great.[14]

We will say no more for now of historical readings, except to caution on the obvious methodological dangers in building an interpretation of a work of fiction on a combination of facts and personages which are themselves a mixture of fiction and history, and indeed involve even then a further mixture of the factual and the anecdotal. This is not, of course, to downplay the role of anecdote and hearsay, or for that matter of history, within *The Queen of Spades* itself.

A number of readings of *The Queen of Spades* concentrate, not surprisingly perhaps, on card games. Nathan Rosen (1975), among others, pays particular attention to the secret of the cards and we shall have occasion to mention his article again. Gukovsky (1957) had stressed the economic subtext to the system of card playing. G.P. Makogonenko (1982: 252) also sees card playing as symbolic of the closed aristocratic social system, particularly in its use in the tale as a circular framing device at the beginning and end of the action: following Hermann's catastrophic loss, we are told, 'the gaming resumed its normal course'. However, an article by Iurii Lotman (1975, English translation 1978), has provided us with by far the strongest reading to have been based on card playing as a modelling system.

Lotman is concerned with cards as a cultural semiotic system, imposing its own conventions and codes of behaviour. Makogonenko (1982: 224 and 227) quotes V.F. Odoevsky's *Russian Nights* on equality in cards as 'Jacobinism in its full beauty' and on cards as masking 'almost all the vicious feelings of man'.[15] For Lotman not only the framing process of card playing but the cyclical repetitions implied in the Conclusion signify victory to an automatic world at the end of a process involving both the vivification of automatism and the paralysis of being. He begins by noting the traditional dual function of cards: for the purposes of gaming and fortune telling. Card games imply modelling systems for conflict situations of bidding and chance, with a mutual influence exerted between the two. In the case of faro, however, the relatively moral element of bidding or calculation is all but eliminated, with the emphasis resting almost solely upon 'chance' (seen as fashionable, dangerous and immoral); indeed, in faro in effect 'the punter is playing [indeed, duelling] not with another person, but with Chance' (Lotman, 1978: 462). The card game of sheer chance is thus seen as a modelling system for the development of Russian society into the 'modern' age. Derzhavin's ode *To Fortune* had portrayed political life as a game of chance and economic prospects were also seen as equally random and chaotic:

> People of the age saw their culture as a contradictory whole, modelled on the high points of life by distinct and intelligible models, but in real life giving the appearance of chaos and the triumph of chance, whose image is the world of the card game of chance. (ibid.: 467)

A radical improvement in status equals a win; the psychological condition of the hero is one of hope; if victory does not ensue, the final loss is one of ruin (or madness: 469); the key factor will be chance. Lotman points to the clash of cultures and generations in Pushkin's story (the 1770s and the 1830s, 'the age of porcelain shepherdesses...and the age of money': 472-3). This leads to the emergence of 'a man of will' (or, as seen by Leatherbarrow, 1985: 13, 'a parody of the romantic man of will'):

> The 'probability' picture of the world, the conception of life as being ruled by Chance, opens before the individual opportunities of unlimited success, and sharply divides people into the passive slaves of circumstance and the 'men of Fate', whose appearance in European

culture in the first half of the nineteenth century is invariably associated with the figure of Napoleon. (Lotman, 1978: 474)

Moreover, the plot is readily reducible to a series of 'games people play': at first Hermann's games of power and love seem to dominate, but subsequently he, like Lizaveta Ivanovna, 'does not know what game the world is playing with him' (477), as the Countess becomes a sign, a playing card, and vice versa.

While Lotman's reading of *The Queen of Spades* may not satisfy totally, and ultimately we must agree with Murav'eva (1977) on the narrowness of Lotman's framework and the dangers inherent in any professed 'key', it must be said that Pushkin's tale is convincingly seen, on one level at least, as emblematic of Russian social and cultural change, with chance playing a dual role, representative both of chaotic elements of the irrational and gaming and of a subversive and progressive agency which undermines and combats entropy.

If Lotman's reading eventually merges the semiotic into the sociological and into the philosophical, Felix Raskolnikoff claims *The Queen of Spades* as a philosophical tale on the Napoleonic theme: Hermann 'retraces "in miniature" the path of Napoleon' in trying conclusions with Fate; his fall represents the triumph of Fate over human will (Raskolnikoff, 1987: 258, 259). Pushkin's interests in the irrational and in Fate are considered a romanticism of a sort, if not the Byronic type. The bulk of the story is seen as a series of omens, prefiguring the fall of Hermann.

A number of critics have followed Vinogradov by attending to narration, style and language in *The Queen of Spades*. Heidi Faletti (1977) follows the Formalist lead into an examination of juxtaposition and sentence structure. John Mersereau has categorised the narrative method employed as that of 'a "told" story, with our conception of Hermann based on judgements provided by the narrator' (Mersereau, 1983: 225). More recently, Brown (1986: 222) says that Pushkin describes actions, rather than thoughts, while Caryl Emerson (1992: 21) has referred to 'a sober, reportorial narrator who documents by the day, hour and minute the uncanny and the mundane with apparently equal confidence'. Vinogradov had discussed the narrator's various poses, of distancing and even possible participation; this approach is followed up by Makogonenko (1982: 213-14) and in considerably further detail by N.K. Gei (1989). According to Justin Doherty (1992: 60), 'while the story's main narrator is a relatively unproblematic figure, the author's is an ironic and teasing voice which upsets and interrupts our attempts to read the text "normally" '; he goes on to cite in this regard the epigraphs, on which we shall have more to say later.

Close reading also leads to detailed studies of the chronology of the tale. Ann Shukman, as part of her almost monographic study of the short story,

If we call the opening scene of Chapter I (i.e. the end of the card game at Narumov's) Day 1, the following pattern emerges:

Note: Upper case letters denote events which are presented to the reader as being in the past, being merely referred to *en passant*. Lower case letters denote those events which are presented to the reader as the present:

Event		Day 1	Order of Presentation
(i)	COUNTESS IS GIVEN SECRET OF 3 CARDS BY ST. GERMAIN	-60 YEARS (APPROX.)	3
(ii)	BIRTH OF CHEKALINSKY	-60 YEARS (APPROX.)	35
(iii)	CHAPLITSKY IS GIVEN SECRET OF 3 CARDS BY COUNTESS	-? YEARS	4
(iv)	DEATH OF COUNTESS'S FRIEND DAR'YA PETROVNA	-7 YEARS (APPROX.)	7
(v)	GERMANN (G) ATTENDS CARD GAMES WITHOUT GAMBLING	-? DAYS	14
(vi)	START OF CARD GAME AT NARUMOV'S	-1 DAY	1
(vii)	End of card game at Narumov's	0 (Day 1)	2&5
(viii)	G. muses on 3 cards anecdote	+1	15
(ix)	Lizaveta (L) sees G. for first time	+2	10&18
(x)	POSSIBLE DATE FOR COUNTESS'S DEATH, GIVEN HER AGE	+3	16
(xi)	L. sees G. for second time	+4 (approx.)	11
(xii)	G. appears daily beneath Countess's windows	+5 to +8	12
(xiii)	ANOTHER POSSIBLE DATE FOR COUNTESS'S DEATH, GIVEN HER AGE	+8	17
(xiv)	BALL ATTENDED BY TOMSKY	+8 to +9	8

(xv)	Countess and Tomsky converse. Tomsky asks for permission to present Narumov to her	+9	6
(xvi)	L. blushes on seeing G.	+9	9
(xvii)	L. smiles at G.	+11	13
(xviii)	L. receives letter from G., and writes answer	+11	19
(xix)	L. gives her answer to G.	+12	20
(xx)	L. returns note asking for assignation	+15	21
(xxi)	L. receives series of letters from G.	+16 to +20 (?)	22
(xxii)	L. finally agress to assignation	+21	23
(xxiii)	G. arrives outside Countess's house	+21	24
(xxiv)	Countess leaves for ball	+21	25
(xxv)	G. enters Countess's house	+21	26
(xxvi)	L. and Tomsky discuss G. at ball	+21	30
(xxvii)	L. and Countess return from ball	+22	27
(xxviii)	G. confronts Countess, who dies	+22	28
(xxix)	L. sits in her room after the ball	+22	29
(xxx)	G. enters L.'s room	+22	31
(xxxi)	G. leaves Countess's house	+22	32
(xxxii)	Funeral of Countess	+25	33
(xxxiii)	Visitation of Countess's ghost	+26	34
(xxxiv)	First game with Chekalinsky	+26 +X	36
(xxxv)	Second game with Chekalinsky	$+26 + (X+1)$	37
(xxxvi)	Third game with Chekalinsky	$+26 + (X+2)$	38
(xxxvii)	Events of conclusion	$+26 + (X+2) +Y$	39

Fig. 2 (Reproduced by permission of Michael Pursglove.)

remarks upon 'the most complex treatment of event time' in *The Queen of Spades* (Shukman, 1977: 39), involving flashback, inversion, shifts of point of view and flashforward, and produces a highly complex diagrammatic illustration of this (ibid.: 46-9). Simpler, and therefore more effective, is the subsequent tabular presentation by Michael Pursglove, in terms of a listing of chronological 'events' (i.e. *fabula*), as opposed to their introduction in the story (i.e. *siuzhet*), along with a calculation of the time elapsed between 'day one' of the action (i.e. the card game at Narumov's) and any given event (Pursglove, 1985: 11-13). Taking this to be the nearest we are likely to see to a definitive representation of the chronological schema behind *The Queen of Spades*, we here take advantage of the author's permission to reproduce this table (see Fig. 2).

Commentators, as we have seen, have long expatiated on the role of numbers in *The Queen of Spades*, from Slonimsky onwards at least, seeing in particular pre-figurings of the 'three-seven-ace' formula within the earlier part of the text. We have also noted the observations on dualities, oppositions and juxtapositions made by various critics (see also Debreczeny, 1983; Pursglove, 1985; and Raskolnikoff, 1987). Bocharov (1978) has also pointed up such things, along with the importance of the numbers 'one' and 'two' (as well as 'three' and 'seven'; see also Falchikov, 1977 on numbers). However, altogether qualitatively different are the researches of Lauren Leighton, over a series of three articles which are best considered together.

We have already made mention of Leighton's article on gematria, embracing also 'logomachy' and cryptography (word-making in general and 'words within words', Leighton, 1977B). In his third article, Leighton himself (1982: 22) deems *The Queen of Spades* to be 'so deliberately ambiguous that the scholarship devoted to it is markedly ingenious'. One may safely say that none is more ingenious than Leighton's own contributions to the critical literature. His other article of 1977 (here termed 'Leighton, 1977A') explores numbers and numerology (the use of three, seven, one and combinations or breakdowns thereof) in almost mind-boggling detail. Numbers in all directions, repetitions, word counts and number counts are employed to demonstrate that the tale is numerically permeated and penetrated to an extent never before suspected in what is seen as 'a carefully devised system' (Leighton, 1977A: 431). Almost anything examined seems to add up to something which at least sounds significant. The announcement early on that the tale comprises 'seven basic parts, each composed of three plot units' (ibid.: 420) is the merest foretaste of what is to come. In his 1982 essay, Leighton strongly endorses Weber's (1968) findings on Freemasonry, adding further details from numerology, description, gesture and phrase detected within the work. As to what should be made of all this, this is a question to which we shall have to return, albeit a trifle peremptorily.

If a numerological reading is ultimately to be seen as a psychological interpretation of the story, then it has to be said that psychological readings have been the common currency of *Queen of Spades* scholarship. These can themselves be subdivided. We have noted a number of what we might describe as Soviet 'materialist' readings (from Lezhnev, Gukovsky and others). However, we can also find a psychological explanation strongly advocated by Western commentators as well. Such a case is cogently put by Mersereau, for instance (1983: 223), who goes as far as to call the central conceivably supernatural event, the posthumous visitation of the Countess to Hermann, not even a hallucination, but a 'dream':[16]

> The content of the dream is thoroughly motivated. The spectre begins with a preamble stating that its appearance is against its will, a fact which Hermann must realize in view of his relationship with the late Countess. The sequence of the winning three cards which she reveals has already been partly established, since Hermann had previously mentioned 'calculation, restraint and industriousness' as the three cards which would *triple* and *make sevenfold* his capital. The ace as the third card is the natural choice of a person suffering from delusions of grandeur: would the great Hermann cap his triumph with a lowly ten or knave? No, the two magical cards, three and seven, are crowned by the ace, with which Hermann identifies personally – in Russian the word ace [*tuz*] refers to a person of particular importance and prestige. Finally, forgiveness is promised if he will marry Lizaveta, a dream admonition developing from his unconscious guilt at having treated Lizaveta in a base and cruel manner.

Much of this is, of course, long familiar and, plausible though such an explication may seem, it still raises, or leaves, as usual, a number of unanswered questions.

An alternative psychological reading, within the terms of what he calls 'neurostructuralism', has been supplied by E.C. Barksdale. This reading shades off into myth and fairy tale, although it is rooted in psychology and ambiguity: 'Pushkin's story is capable of a special type of ambiguity which makes every line appear as a contributory factor to a long double helix of truth and falsehood' (Barksdale, 1979: 78). This assertion is based upon the absence of personality in the narrator and in particular upon the observation that Pushkin's figures are without an 'engram' encoded into their psyches, meaning that, of the characters in *The Queen of Spades*, only the Countess has any recollections and in her case 'the totality of her experience is time which has passed' (ibid.: 79). The basic duality of the story for Barksdale (the alternation between occult and quotidien) derives therefore from the absence of conscious memory in the characters, who become merely 'a series of types'; given the elimination of narratorial personality, 'as little is known of the characters' real motivations as is known of their memories' (81). The resultant creation is that of 'one myth, vast and meaningful because it has so little meaning' (82).

The other type of psychological reading, developed so far only in Western criticism, is of the psychoanalytical or Freudian variety. Touches of this have been suggested by Debreczeny (1977 and 1983: 232-8, the latter, from his book on Pushkin's prose, being the lengthiest treatment of *The Queen of Spades* up to this point in English); in Rosen's comments on self-punishment motivating Hermann's final disaster (Rosen, 1975: 267); and in the comments by Briggs (1983) and others on the degree to which overt or covert sexual innuendo permeates the tale. Attempts at avowedly psychoanalytical readings have been made by Murray and Albert Schwartz (1975) and Adele Barker (1984), talking of Hermann's 'unresolved Oedipal fixation' (Barker, 1984: 202). The Countess is naturally enough seen as a mother figure. Much is made of the father's legacy and of father figures (Saint-Germain, Cheka-linsky), of Hermann's old nurse (confirming his infantilism), his unloaded gun (crudely suggesting impotence) and the magnificent flower of his dream (signifying female genitals).[17] Hermann's final error can be seen as arising from guilt over Oedipal ties, while the themes of money and greed as sexual substitute, love and death, and madness all seem more or less to fit.

If a 'vulgar Freudian' reading, not unlike the 'vulgar Marxist' variety, seems both limited and predictable, there are undeniably elements within the story which indeed provoke psychoanalytical types of analysis and we shall look again at such an approach in Part Two of this study.

Meanwhile, the first reading of a Lacanian variety appeared in 1992, written by Alfred Thomas. Thomas sees little value in the 'biological-based approach' of existing psychoanalytical studies in which, in place of Freud's author-based model of 'psychobiography', 'the vulgar Freudians privilege the hero as the centre of the psychoedipal drama' (Thomas, 1992: 48). Such studies take little account of 'the interlocking pattern of coincidences and repetitions, ...the elaborate numerological structure' (ibid.: 49). Instead, Thomas wishes to 'argue that madness should not be sought within the mental condition of any one character, but is a projection of a psychosis immanent in the text itself'; in other words he proposes a model of 'text as psyche' (ibid.). What basically happens in the story, according to Thomas, is a repetition in scene after scene of 'a primal trauma where the hero is confronted with the spectre of an unresolvable enigma' (ibid.): the secret of the three cards, which is continually deferred from one authority to another, from the 'primal' story within a story onwards, but with no resolution from Hermann's standpoint, as it is not divulged to him and he in any case 'remains deaf to its secret meaning' (51). There ensues a repetition of voyeuristic scenes, 'deaf exchange' conversations, 'active–passive' oppositions and an

inability to articulate the impossible object of desire. It is Hermann's un-
awareness of this impossibility which causes his madness. The number three,
Thomas reminds us (56), its other connotations apart, 'is also descriptive of
the oedipal triangle':

> The numerological determinants of German [sic]'s unreason are al-
> ready present, woven into the text from the beginning to the end. In
> this sense, German is akin to an antique hero, an Oedipus deaf to the
> laughter of the Gods. (58)

A number of commentators have always been ready to argue for a fully blown
supernatural explanation. Most notably perhaps Kodjak (in his 1976 article)
is able to contend quite plausibly, from the text itself, that Hermann was by
no means necessarily still in an inebriated state at the time of his 'visitation'
from the Countess. He also reminds us that the numbers three and seven have
an independent derivation from the gambling process associated with faro
(see Chkhaidze, 1960) and are not therefore dependent for their introduction
into the tale on Hermann's psyche. He also (again from a close reading of
the text) claims the narrator as a 'witness' to Hermann receiving his visitation
(Kodjak, 1976: 102-3). From his analysis of the tale, based on what he calls
'gambling sign', 'narrator sign', 'ghost sign' and 'Faust sign' systems, he
reads into the story a supernatural tale of Faustian bargaining. Nathan Rosen
(1975) also wishes to argue for supernatural elements, but seemingly within
a total explanation that places strong weight too on the psychological. Others
to opt strongly for the supernatural, in the manner of Labriolle (1969),
include Diana Burgin (1974) and Michael Falchikov (1977).

Once the supernatural is admitted, however, it seldom knows where to
stop and it is frequently accompanied, as we have seen, by a willingness to
go outside the text, or to build entire edifices from the merest textual bricks
and with imaginary mortar between them. Thus Kodjak (1976: 103) sees
Hermann's role in his confrontation with the Countess as 'the angel of death',
somehow fusing with Saint-Germain, 'the midnight bridegroom'; the Countess (see ibid.: 105-10), it is argued, expects a nocturnal visitor in fulfilment
of her covenant made with Saint-Germain sixty years ago. However, apart
from any other objection (such as the lack of evidence for this), why should
the day in question be thought to be exactly sixty years on, to the night, even
if there really would be any significance in this? The probability of a sexual
liaison in 'reality' between the Countess and Saint-Germain is guessed at, or
even assumed, by a number of commentators. Thus Burgin takes Chaplitsky
to be the Countess's 'natural' son by Saint-Germain and subsequently
perhaps her lover, as part of an 'erotic cabal' (Burgin, 1974: 50-2). Barker
(1984: 203) reads Tomsky's anecdote as suggesting that 'the countess might
have taken the young Chaplitsky as her lover'. W.W. Rowe (1988: 150), on

the other hand, thinks that Chekalinsky might be a natural son of the Countess. According to Gareth Williams (1981: 211), 'if the reader wishes to make this interpretation', Saint-Germain may have possessed the elixir of life and may actually be Chekalinsky. Speculation may also centre on Tomsky and even Narumov. We shall, once again, return to this approach when we come to attempt an assessment of various possible readings of *The Queen of Spades* in Part Two.

Critics wishing to give equal rein to the psychological and the super-natural opt for a reading which stresses ambiguity. This approach has gained considerable currency in Soviet and Russian criticism over the past two decades (Poliakova, 1974; Murav'eva, 1978), as well as in Western commentaries (Shukman, 1977; Phillips, 1982; Leatherbarrow, 1985; Williams, 1989; as well as the overall interpretation implicit in Rosen, 1975). A slightly more specialised form of ambiguity has been developed as the 'fantastic' interpretation, based on Dostoevsky's lead (and using Todorov's theory, or developments thereof) and dependent ultimately on reader hesitation up to (and even beyond) the very end (see for instance Reeder, 1982; Davydov, 1987; and Cornwell, 1990).[18] Some of the arguments for this type of reading will be adduced later.

We have already mentioned fairy tale in passing. However, several critics have noticed the manner in which *The Queen of Spades* seems to fit the structure of the fairy (or folk) tale, in terms of its plot functions and characters, as detailed by the Formalist theorist Vladimir Propp.[19] This was first shown by Ann Shukman (1977) and in Russia by N.N. Petrunina (1980), given the presence within the story of a quest, secret knowledge, the prize of riches and/or a fair maiden, a donor, an assistant, fatal choices, mistakes and so on. Such a scheme has been developed in order to compare *The Queen of Spades* with other works (see Reeder, 1982, who does a Hoffmann comparison; and Cornwell, 1990, who compares Pushkin's story with *The Aspern Papers* by Henry James) and the plot segments or functions can easily be tabulated, to illustrate their fairy-tale proximity, as will be shown subsequently.

A fairy tale reading is naturally able to absorb the supernatural without any fear of hindrance or embarrassment. Neither does a parodic reading have to concern itself with watertight explanations in terms of this or another world. In the view of A.D.P. Briggs (1983: 224), 'if *The Queen of Spades* has parodied the cheap tale of the supernatural it has done so in the most effective way, by demonstrating how a good one should be written'. Nevertheless, there is of course far more than 'the cheap tale' to *The Queen of Spades*, by most interpretations. A number of critics, from Lezhnev in 1937, have been willing to countenance a multiplicity of interpretations. Kodjak (1976: 115) sees it as implying a 'theological vision of the world', a Mephistophelian 'picture of pervasive evil'. To Debreczeny (1983: 200) the question as to

Fig. 3 Russian playing cards, ca. 1830 (reproduced by permission of Nathan Rosen; Courtesy of the Trustees of the British Museum).

whether the Countess' ghost 'really' visited Hermann is simply 'as irrelevant as asking whether [Kafka's] Gregor Samsa could *really* have turned into a huge cockroach', as 'the meaning of imaginative literature is conveyed through its system of symbols' (ibid.: 201), irrespective of any 'immediate correspondence to scientifically verifiable reality'. This seems, in essence, no different from the 'fairy-tale' position.

Two recent articles also see Pushkin's tale ultimately as an amalgam of literary devices. Doherty (1992: 51), who also makes use of fairy tale, talks of 'Pushkin's "ludic" attitude', in tune of course with the theme and discourse of card playing, within a 'self-conscious text' (ibid.: 62), which, from a parody of the fantastic tale, becomes 'something more like a parody of writing, reading and critical interpretation'. If for Doherty (ibid.) the tale may be a text 'which may in the end be "about" nothing', then for Emerson too the key word may be *shutka* (joke): for 'in *real* gambling...there *is no system*' (Emerson, 1992: 25; her emphasis). Pushkin in this story 'teases the reader with partial keys', so that the work becomes 'an allegory of interpretation itself' (ibid.: 25, 26). Having arrived at such a metafictional, indeed deconstructivist position, it may seem that the full gamut has been run: there is nowhere further for *Queen of Spades* criticism to go. However, to believe this would be to believe that literary criticism in general has run its full course and to bet perhaps over heavily, and over Hermann-like, against the continued ingenuity of critical scholarship.

Notes to Part One

1. On the opera libretto adaptations, see Roberts, 1979. Cinematic adaptations too came in the twentieth century: an early Russian cinematic version was followed by the British film *The Queen of Spades*, directed by Thorold Dickinson (1948, in black and white), starring Anton Walbrook and Edith Evans.

2. On French translations, in particular that of Prosper Mérimée, see Henry, 1987; and Bobrova, 1958. For a note of early English translations, see Cornwell, 1990: 240 n.13; an even earlier one (of 1850) is noted by Gilbert Phelps in his *The Russian Novel in English Fiction* (Hutchinson: London, 1956) 16; for more recent English translations see Bibliography.

3. Tzvetan Todorov's *Introduction à la littérature fantastique* (Editions du Seuil: Paris, 1970) cites Dostoevsky in other respects; Rosemary Jackson notes this statement by Dostoevsky in her *Fantasy: The Literature of Subversion* (Methuen: London and New York, 1981); see also Cornwell, 1990: 23 and 113-21.

4. I quote here from the original (Shklovskii, 1937), as the English translation (Shklovsky, 1976) turns out to have been somewhat savagely cut.

5. An earlier linguistic analyst, M.O. Lopatto (in 1918) had established that *The Queen of Spades* comprises 40% verbs, 44% nouns and only 16% adjectives and adverbs (Vinogradov, 1980: 227).

6. Debreczeny, 1983 (323 n.31) later disputes with Alekseev that 'Pushkin uses the terms *magnetizm* and *galvanizm*...in a purely scientific sense, in keeping with the education and perception of Hermann'.

7. For an even more detailed account, see Nabokov, 1964: 258-61. On this and cards generally in the period, see Lotman, 1978, a seminal article to which we shall return.

8. Later examinations of Hoffmann's impact on *The Queen of Spades* do not have much more to contribute in this respect: see Ingham, 1974; Botnikova, 1977; Reeder, 1982, who sees Pushkin as producing a parody of a composite Hoffmann tale, we shall have cause to mention later in other connections. Similarly, von Gronicka, 1968: 67, in his examination of Goethe in Russian literature, sees *The Queen of Spades* as 'if anything, a parody of Goethe's immortal creation' (i.e. of *Faust*); Kodjak, 1976 will have rather more to say on this matter.

9. Labriolle claims (265 n.7) that such an interpretation had been intuited

by Gershenzon (1919), as what would have been the case had Pushkin been writing a French freneticist novel, but rejected for the actual Pushkin as too 'vulgar'. Neither Labriolle nor a number of subsequent commentators, as we shall see, were to be so squeamish.

10. Russian prose genre terminology does not exactly match that of English (compare for that matter the nuances of the French *conte* and *nouvelle*). *Roman* is normally equivalent to 'novel'. *Povest'* (a long tale or typically a short novel) can sometimes exceed the length of shorter *romany*, in which case the distinguishing factor would normally lie in its more limited timescale and/or its unilinear plot. *Rasskaz* is a plain 'short story' (sometimes in Russian literature very short); *skazka* is a 'fairy tale'; *novella* (a term less used in Russian criticism) is given this particular definition by Seleznev. For a discussion of such terms (other than in Russian literature), see Ian Reid, *The Short Story* (Methuen: London, 1977).

11. On Balzac's *La Peau de chagrin*, see Gregg, 1966; Kupreanova, 1981: 306, reiterates the Balzac and Stendhal connections; on Hoffmann, see note 8 above; Kodjak, 1976 explores the Faustian bargain; Busch, 1987 examines French freneticism in general, while Williams, 1981 looks more closely at Janin. *Spader Dame* was first noted by Nabokov, 1964, 3: 97 and is subsequently taken up by Clayton, 1974; Sharypkin, 1974; and V. Nabokov and Barabtarlo, 1991.

12. Curiously, the British scholar C.R. Pike, in an unpublished paper, speculates that Hermann might be an 'ex-Decembrist?', though without stating his reasoning for such a suggestion. Leighton (1977B: 468 n.32) thinks that Ryleev is a partial prototype for Hermann.

13. See Andrej Kodjak, *Pushkin's I.P. Belkin* (Slavica: Columbus, Ohio, 1979). Interestingly, in his 1976 article on *The Queen of Spades*, Kodjak takes the Faustian rather than the Decembrist trail.

14. Unfortunately Hubbs does not improve her argument by getting a number of the details of the story wrong (including even the order in which the cards are to be played, stated as 'three-one-seven' (Hubbs, 1988: 221). Lerner had also added Voltaire into the historico-literary equation (as later does Williams, 1981 etc.), by means of his ode on Catherine II's carousel, built in 1766 with the participation of Chernysheva (just before her marriage to Golitsyn: Lerner, 1929: 147 n.1); Lerner also provides the fact that Golitsyna's great-nephew Count Z.G. Chernyshev was a Decembrist exiled to Siberia (ibid.: 157). Other figures brought in to such discussions include Fonvizin, whose meeting with Saint-Germain in 1778 was apparently known to Pushkin and, at the contemporary end, Mickiewicz, with whom *The Bronze Horseman* was allegedly not Pushkin's only polemic (see Shvartsband, 1988: 156, 154).

15. Odoevsky is also quoted on the use of the fantastic (Makogonenko, 1982: 205; see Odoevsky, *Russian Nights*, Nauka: Leningrad, 1975: 189).

Odoevsky was the one literary figure of the Romantic period to be consistently opposed to card-playing: see Neil Cornwell, *V.F. Odoyevsky: His life, times and milieu* (Athlone Press: London, 1986, *passim.*); and in particular the story 'Skazka o tom, po kakomu sluchaiu kollezhskomu sovetniku Ivanu Bogdanovichu Otnosheniiu ne udalos' v svetloe voskresen'e pozdravit' svoikh nachal'nikov s prazdnikom', in V.F. Odoyevsky, *Pyostryye skazki*, edited by Neil Cornwell (Durham Modern Language Series: University of Durham, 1988).

16. Mersereau is not alone in this. See also Katz, 1980, who makes the Russian division between sleep-dream and day-dream in the tale (*son* and *mechta*); Briggs, 1983; Barker, 1984; Remizov, 1989: 148-9, who seems to see much of the tale as a dream; and Thomas, 1992.

17. There is at least one occasion when Schwartz and Schwartz are misled by their reliance on Pushkin's text in translated form: the idea that 'money will not "slip through [Hermann's] fingers" ' suggests to them a 'masturbatory fantasy' (1975: 283); in the Russian original (Pushkin, 1948: 241), *ne berech'* means merely 'not to take care of'.

18. See also Žekulin:,1987, who uses Todorov, Jackson (see note 3 above) and a PhD dissertation by Nancy Traill. A slightly different form of fantastic theory is used by Iu. Mann (1978: 67), who applies his concept of the 'veiled' fantastic to *The Queen of Spades*, in which the fantastic or supernatural events are relegated from the foreground to the pre-history of a work, or (appropriately enough) to hearsay.

19. See V. Propp, *Morphology of the Folktale*, translated by Laurence Scott, 2nd edn (University of Texas Press: Austin and London, 1968 and reprintings).

Part Two

Commentary to
The Queen Of Spades

Chapter I

The first thing the reader notices on turning to *The Queen of Spades*, the title apart, are the first two of its seven epigraphs: to the work as a whole and to Chapter I. A growing literature exists on the epigraphs, to which we may refer from time to time (see particularly, however, the articles by Gareth Williams). The initial epigraph, which seems to set the tone for the work, reads 'from the latest fortune-telling book': 'The queen of spades signifies secret malice'. The epigraph to Chapter I,[1] marked 'manuscript ballad' in a rough copy, is by Pushkin himself, probably written about 1828, and is an obvious parody of the agitational songs for which Ryleev and Bestuzhev were well known up until the events of 14 December 1825. The impact of these epigraphs together is likely to have suggested to the reader of the day a combination of superstitious foreboding and political gambling, while also implying an atmosphere of tension and drama in a setting of inclement weather.

Much of this is almost immediately confirmed in the opening paragraph, with its no-nonsense, straight down to business start (and especially the 'long winter night'[2] of the second sentence: 227:15). The first sentence is one of the most famous beginnings in Russian literature (reminding later readers of the opening of Tolstoy's *Anna Karenina*, which in turn derived its inspiration from an earlier Pushkin prose fragment). The first sentence, as noted in Part One, has no personal pronoun in the original and could therefore imply either 'we' (inclusive of its narrator) or an exclusive 'they'. A sense of action is immediately conveyed, which turns very quickly into dialogue.

The first name mentioned (apart from Narumov's in the first sentence) is that of one Surin – one of the 'young people' (230:7) who have gathered at Narumov's, quite naturally addressed as 'Surin' (227:20), but a personage whose name never recurs. His modest gambling is of no lasting interest, and merely a conversational gambit to facilitate the introduction to us of Hermann,[3] whose gambling habits (or rather the lack of them) soon prove to be of crucial importance. 'One of the guests' (227:26) first draws attention to Hermann's allegedly never having gambled with a card in his life; Hermann's own facility for epigrammatic speech is immediately displayed, but it is Tomsky who tells us that 'Hermann is German: he's calculating and that's all there is to it!' (227:33). Given the partial, and less than total, picture of Hermann that is conveyed here, we may regard this statement as a pointer to the possibility that less than total reliability may be expected in Tomsky's own anecdote, which is about to follow.

Tomsky's anecdote is, of course, crucial for everything that follows in *The Queen of Spades*: without Tomsky's anecdote of the secret of the three cards, supposedly revealed to the Countess by the Count Saint-Germain, there would be no tale. 'And indeed was any secret revealed to her?' asks John Bayley (1971: 319). This is indeed the vital question. There are at least two apparent contradictions within Tomsky's narrative, which is delivered (through what the Russian Formalists called *skaz*, 'style': very much his own words), in a polished story-telling manner, which includes details that he may have been told (but cannot possibly have known) and which sound very much like hearsay, family tradition, elaboration or even invention. He introduces the subject by declaring that he cannot understand why his grandmother no longer bets (227:34-5); although we are not told specifically that there was an interdiction on her repeating the operation, there certainly is said to have been such a thing in the case of Chaplitsky (230:1-2). It should therefore not be a surprise to Tomsky that she did not, or could not, do it again; it seems rather that he wished to introduce the subject for conversational or, possibly even, more dubious motives. Secondly, the Countess is told by Saint-Germain: 'You don't need any money for this' (229:13); one wonders therefore how she manages to punt against the Duke of Orleans without having brought with her the sum that she owes and to start off betting with a sum sufficient to win back all her previous immense loss in the space of three cards.

Brief historical notes on all these figures (the Duc de Richelieu etc.) and the gambling terms employed may be found in Forsyth's Russian language edition and as notes to Debreczeny's English translation (see Bibliography) and will not generally be repeated here unless deemed absolutely necessary; a longer note is however here provided on Saint-Germain, who is of special importance. It is also probably essential at this point to include in this digression a brief description of how the game of faro was played.

Faro (or pharaon: pharoah's heads were on the cards at some earlier stage) was one of the most popular gambling games among the European aristocracy in the eighteenth and early nineteenth centuries. It was a game, to all intents and purposes, of pure chance, with virtually no element of skill or bluff (unlike, say, whist). The banker held the bank against any number of punters (although in the no doubt unusually big and dramatic games played or alluded to in *The Queen of Spades* one punter only bets against the bank). Two packs of cards were used. From one pack, the punter would select a card and place it face down on the table. He/she would put on a stake by placing money on top of the card, or by writing the sum staked on it in chalk. The banker would then begin dealing cards from the other pack in pairs, placing them face up on either side of the punter's card. If, or when, the punter's card made a double (i.e. matched) the card which fell to the right, the banker won the stake; if it corresponded with the one to the left, the punter won. A punter could double the stake by bending back a corner of his/her card and double that by bending back a second corner. Because of the stakes involved, and to be sure there could be no marked cards, in *The Queen of Spades* new packs were unsealed and used each time. For a diagrammatic representation of Hermann's three games, see Figure 1.

Returning to the anecdote, we may note that Tomsky gives us a flavour both of Saint-Germain's reputation as an occultist and as a charlatan or spy (228:36-7). The alternatives are immediately there. We are also told of his 'very respectable appearance' (228:38) and (perhaps with tongue in cheek) that 'grandmother still loves him to distraction' (228:39-40). At this point, in which direct speech has featured between the Countess and Saint-Germain, the latter imparts a 'secret' [*taina*] to the former by indirect speech (229:14). 'Secret' is obviously a key word in *The Queen of Spades* and, upon its introduction, it is referred to by indeterminate means, less specific than the immediate context of anecdote and dialogue might have warranted. There is then an apparently narratorial intervention into Tomsky's anecdote: 'The young gamblers doubled their attention. Tomsky lit his pipe, took a puff, and continued' (229:16-17). Such as we (and the surrounding audience of 'young gamblers') are to know of the secret emerges then in Tomsky's continued narrative; we are merely told that 'grandmother completely won back her losses' against the Duke by playing three cards which she had chosen, one after the other (229:21-3). We are not told which cards. However, had such an event happened (or, when allegedly it did, according to society anecdotage on which this society anecdote was itself probably at least partly based), it seems highly likely that the winning cards would have been identified and memorised by witnesses.

Strangely, the audience of young gamblers do not even ask whether it is known what the cards were. As if entering into the anecdotal spirit of Tomsky's own narrative presentation, they instead hazard guesses as to an explanation of this phenomenal incident. The ways in which they do this, and even perhaps the fact of their doing this, open up a whole range of interpretations for the tale as a whole: what we might call the micro-anecdote within the whole macro-anecdote has embedded within it, by the 'greater narrator' and by means of listeners' reactions, a *mise en abyme* for the 'greater tale'.[4] Thus the following hares are loosed, which may be traced or chased by readers and critics through the remainder of the tale: 'Chance!', which is said by 'one of the guests' (229:24). 'Fairy tale!', as remarked by

Hermann (229:25). A 'third' suggests that 'powdered cards' (in other words, fraudulent play) may have been involved (229:26). This immediately brings a 'self-important' response of 'I don't think so' from Tomsky (229:27). There is in fact, by implication at least, a fourth reply (noted by Shvartsband, 1988: 163): Narumov expresses surprise that Tomsky should not have 'taken over' these 'cabalistics' from his grandmother (229:29-30). Tomsky replies that she had 'four inveterate gamblers' as sons, including his own father, to whom she 'did not reveal her secret' (229:31-2), suggesting a negative balance, or even a denial, of the four suggested explanations.

In fact nothing in *The Queen of Spades* is ever as simple as it might seem. The three answers, picked up by many critics, have already now become four and close inspection reveals further possibilities, owing to ambiguity, in the first two at least. 'Chance' (*sluchai*) may connote either mild coincidence or perhaps a more guided stroke of fate, but in any event provides a rational explanation of a sort (if only of, to a greater or lesser extent, an irrational sort; for a disquisition on chance in relation to Pushkin, see Abram Terts, 1975: 37-40). 'Fairy tale' (*skazka*) may indicate dismissal as nonsense or, on the other hand, a magical quality of charm or presence (or even be taken literally). Already we have a number of possible interpretations of *The Queen of Spades* here in embryo. 'Powdered cards' may be not on literally, but the possibility of some sort of fraud or hoax remains, despite Tomsky's disavowal (even if Tomsky were deemed to be reliable, he could well be denying only the literal marked card variant of fraud). Cabalistics (*kabalistika*) raises the possibility of serious magic or supernatural involvement, beyond the perhaps more juvenile level of 'fairy tale'.

In any case, Hermann may well have intended the nonsense connotation of *skazka* as his initial reaction (or at least that of fairyland impossibility). Only subsequently, as his obsession develops over the ensuing days (see Fig. 2 for a chronological table of the work), does the magical element of *skazka* sink fully into his 'fiery imagination' (235:22) and turn into something like full cabalistics, with hints even of Faustian bargains (see in particular Kodjak, 1976). This is perhaps the first instance in the tale of Hermann choosing the wrong alternative.

Back again to the anecdote and Tomsky relates the second instance of the secret being employed, which perhaps caused Hermann to take it (even) more seriously. The Countess 'somehow took pity on Chaplitsky' (229:39-40). Strangely, however, the 'rules' seem to have evolved (as they will continue to do, as we shall see in Chapter V): Chaplitsky has to play his three cards one after the other, but he also had 'extracted from him his word of honour never to play in future' (230:1-2). We do not know whether his later demise, 'in poverty, having squandered millions' (229:36-7), followed from any subsequent disregard of this injunction, but it would seem not improbable that it did (but here we are already in danger of making guesses from beyond the text!).

No further responses or discussions are reported: the anecdote concludes and the 'young people' rapidly disperse, or, more exactly, are dispensed with by the overall narrator.

Chapter II

The epigraph to Chapter II (231:2-6), in French and from a 'society conversation', derives (it has been known since Pushkin's own time) from the contemporary poet Denis Davydov (Debreczeny, 1983: 193).[5] As usual too this epigraph seems to have only an oblique relevance to what follows. It prefigures Hermann's unsurprising sexual preference for Lizaveta Ivanovna over the Countess (though, once again, things are never that simple). Of course, Lizaveta is not a mere *suivante* (maid); however, the fact of her not being so may conjure speculation as to exactly who she might be. C.R. Pike notes the use of this epigraph as evidence of Pushkin's 'clique-centrism' and speculates also that it might be intended to refer to physical hygiene.[6]

Chapter II starts off by referring to 'The old Countess ***' (231:7), which is slightly mystifying given that we have already heard of her as 'Countess Anna Fedotovna' (227:35); we also know that Tomsky is descended from his grandmother through the male line (229:32). Kodjak (1976: 99) adduces thus that she must be Countess [*Grafinia*] Tomskaia; some critics merely assume it automatically (e.g. Makogonenko, 1982). The Countess has a bonnet of 'fiery coloured ribbons' (231:9), even before we hear of Hermann's 'fiery imagination' (235:22); she is sitting in her dressing room, with three maids dancing attendance on her and in the company of her 'ward' (*vospitannitsa*, 231:14). The latter, introduced first as a 'young lady' (*baryshnia*, 231:14), is then addressed by the incoming Tomsky, who wishes to present 'one of my friends' to the Countess at a ball the following Friday (231:19), as 'mademoiselle Lise' (231:16) and by the Countess familiarly as 'Lizan'ka' (232:3), before her name emerges as Lizaveta Ivanovna (232:5-6). Society chit-chat gives way to a brief conversation between Lizaveta and Tomsky (known to his grandmother as 'Paul'). Like the reader, Lizaveta wants to know whom Tomsky wishes to present to his grandmother. It is, for some undisclosed reason, Narumov (232:8), host of the card game and a cavalry officer. Lizaveta seemingly expected him to be an engineer (232:11; we already know from Chapter I that Hermann is an engineer, 227:27). Engineers, like Russified Germans, are somewhat inferior socially to fully Russian (and normally aristocratic) cavalry officers, or hussars. Lizaveta, then, has a secret of her own, which will emerge soon enough.

There then follows the richly ironic conversation (given the literary context and her approaching fate) between the Countess and Tomsky on novels, displaying her squeamishness regarding novels in which fathers and mothers are strangled or which feature drowned bodies. The extended meaning of *roman* in Russian, as story or erotic scandal, provides an additional frisson. Tomsky is clearly wrong, or evasive at best, in declaring that 'there are no such novels now' (232:20), in view of the stream of Gothic, horror and frenetic romantic literature which continued to flood Europe. He is correct though in suggesting the availability by this period of Russian novels (and indeed scandals). Point of view then switches to Lizaveta Ivanovna and we first become aware of a 'young officer' in the vicinity of the house (232:28). A conversation then takes place between the demanding Countess and Lizaveta, whose mind is on other things.

This is interrupted by the arrival of books (232:37) from 'Prince Pavel Aleksandrovich' (Tomsky). The narratorial reticence over names is here highlighted by what appears at least to be an inconsistency. As the Countess holds the title 'Countess' (*grafinia* in Russian) and we know that Tomsky is her grandson by the male line, then it should follow, just as her surname should be 'Tomskaia', so should his title be 'Count' (*graf*), rather than 'Prince' (*kniaz'*). It is possible to construct a rudimentary Tomsky family tree, which should go as follows:

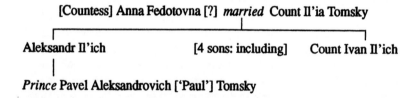

[Countess] Anna Fedotovna [?] *married* Count Il'ia Tomsky

Aleksandr Il'ich   [4 sons: including]   Count Ivan Il'ich

Prince Pavel Aleksandrovich ['Paul'] Tomsky

Why then should Tomsky be a 'prince'? There can be no definitive answer to this question, although it is adduced by some commentators as evidence of a 'mysterious' quality to Tomsky (e.g. Žekulin, 1987). The title of prince is uttered again shortly by the Countess herself (233:9). Kodjak (1976: 99) seems to argue that the title *kniaz'* is used for Tomsky to 'disassociate' him sonically from 'the three characters directly connected with the secret of the three magic cards': the Count Saint-Germain (*graf Sen-Zhermen*), the Countess (*grafinia* ***) and Hermann (*Germann*). If this sounds a little far-fetched, at least the title 'Countess' might be a positive hint of her connection, at whatever level (social, sexual or occult) with the 'Count' (a fictitious title anyway?) Saint-Germain. Another factor to bear in mind is the title of the Countess' supposed prototype, Princess Golitsyna, which may account for Pushkin's having allowed 'Princess' to be ascribed to the Countess on occasion in the first edition of the tale (corrected in the book edition). The alteration may have been caused by Pushkin's attempted cover-up of the Countess' 'true' identity (as suggested by Vera Nabokov, 1991: 51) and there could always lurk the possibility of an undisclosed second marriage entered into at some stage by the Countess.[7]

The conversation is eventually concluded in such a way as to illustrate the capriciousness of the old Countess and the manner in which Lizaveta Ivanovna is put upon. The predicament of the 'poor ward' is rubbed in by a rough quote from Dante: 'Bitter is another's bread, says Dante, and hard are the steps of another's porch' (233:29-30). This comes from *Paradiso* (Canto XVII, ll. 58-60), which in full translation reads 'Thou shalt prove how salt is the taste of another man's bread and how hard is the way up and down another man's stairs'; the stairs seem to foreshadow Hermann's entry to and exit from the Countess' house in Chapters III and IV, while the continuation might almost be a prophecy both of Lizaveta's near 'fall' (had Hermann in fact joined forces and seduced her) and indeed of Hermann's actual fate:

> And that which shall weigh heaviest on thy shoulders is the wicked and senseless company with which thou shalt fall into that valley, which shall become wholly ungrateful, quite mad and furious against thee; but before long they, not thou, shall have the brows red for this. Of their brutish folly their doings shall give proof, so that it shall be to thine honour to have made a party by thyself.[8]

This may be read in varying ways, with Lizaveta, Hermann or for that matter the Countess in mind.

The narration then clinically conveys seemingly dispassionate information about the whims, lifestyle and establishment of the Countess and the exploitation and drudgery of Lizaveta, who is awaiting a 'deliverer' (234:15). We are then told how, two days after the card game and 'a week before the scene' just described (234:23 – see chronology, Fig. 2), Lizaveta noticed a 'young engineer' (234:25-6) staring at her window. Thus begins the process of Hermann's 'courtship', presented at first through Lizaveta's viewpoint: she sees that 'his face is covered by a beaver collar: his black eyes sparkled from under his cap' (234:37-8). This information is conveyed by narratorial 'free indirect discourse' (or 'dual voice'), at the same time through Lizaveta's viewpoint, as their 'unconventional relations' are established (235:6). He is referred to as a 'young man' (235:8), the only indication provided as to his age. Lizaveta is concerned that, by her precipitate question about engineers, she might have betrayed her 'secret' (the second secret of the tale) to 'the frivolous Tomsky' (235:15).

We are next provided with narratorial information about Hermann: 'the son of a Russified German, who left him a small sum in capital' (235:16-17). We are told of his frugal lifestyle, but also of his 'strong passions and fiery imagination' (235:21-2). His cautious conduct and the fact that he, 'being a gambler in his soul, had never had a card in his hand' (235:23-4), is reported by the narrator, as is his stock and emphasised saying of refusing 'to sacrifice the essential in the hope of gaining the superfluous' (235:25-6). Yet he watched card games obsessively. The anecdote of the three cards has an ever greater effect on him and he begins to (day)dream (i.e. evolve the *mechta*) of acquiring the secret from the Countess. By now the narrative has switched directly into the thoughts of Hermann; he then thinks of the tactic of becoming her lover, but thinks there may not be time for that, since 'she is eighty-seven years of age' (235:35-6). We have only Hermann's 'word' for this exact age (noted by Williams, 1981: 213; and 1983: 386-7) and Hermann's susceptibility to the number seven may play a part here. He again ostensibly rejects belief in the anecdote, declaring: 'No! thrift, moderation and diligence: these are my three true cards, this is what will triple and increase sevenfold my capital and bring me peace and independence!' (235:37-40). As we have seen in Part One, it has long been pointed out that Hermann foreshadows here the three and the seven, at least, of his magic numbers to be.[9]

Hermann has now found himself outside what turns out to be the Countess' house, amid the social whirl of a typical aristocratic residence. Obsessed further by the anecdote, he returns late to 'his humble corner' (236:12-13) to dream (this time the somnolent *son*) of cards and of pocketing his wondrous winnings) (Terts, 1975: 36, calls him 'the pocketer Hermann' [*karmannik Germann*]). On awakening, he determines to realise his dream (in both senses) and 'an unknown force, it seemed, drew him' again to the Countess' house (236:19-20; to whom did it 'seem'? asks Gei, 1989: 185). Now, from Hermann's viewpoint, we hear of the 'fresh face [*les fraîches?*] and black eyes' of Lizaveta (236:23). 'That minute decided his fate', we are told (236:23-4). It may indeed have done; however, that statement is just as open to a plurality of meanings as is much else in the tale. No conclusions should be jumped to as to Hermann's supposed 'love' for Lizaveta; it is probable that in her he merely spotted a rather more promising tactic than endeavouring to make love to her octogenarian benefactress.

Chapter III

The epigraph to Chapter III is once again in French ('*Vous m'écrivez, mon ange, des lettres de quatre pages plus vite que je ne puis les lire*', attributed to 'Correspondence', 237:1-4), is probably Pushkin's own invention (it is a variation on one used in an earlier prose fragment) and again it bears only oblique relevance to what follows: Hermann does write letters to Lizaveta. At first she tries not to read them, but subsequently becomes his reluctant reader and clandestine correspondent. She at first responds negatively, but he eventually receives a letter from her setting up an assignation. It may be noteworthy that Hermann's letters are only briefly outlined (twice), while this is counter-balanced by the text of two of those written by Lizaveta Ivanovna.

Chapter III opens as a continuation of the main scene of Chapter II, in which another virtually deaf dialogue is taking place between the Countess and Lizaveta Ivanovna; once again Lizaveta is preoccupied with her secret and it is the deaf Countess who has trouble making herself heard or noticed. The first half of the chapter features an embedded epistolary exchange between the two. However, just like the budding love affair itself, these occurrences are dwarfed by the dramatic events which they set in motion. Hermann's first letter is a declaration of love 'taken word for word from a German novel' (237:23-4).[10] This fact goes unrecognised by Lizaveta. Alarmed, Lizaveta is at the same time flattered and, sensing perhaps a potential 'deliverer', decides to reply. Her answer is suitably remonstrative, without slamming the door.

Hermann persists with further letters, no longer translated from German but now written 'inspired by passion' (238:34-5). This has occasionally been taken to mean that Hermann is now genuinely in love with Lizaveta; it seems more likely, however, that money is still the motivating passion (rather than sexual desire) and that Hermann's 'unbridled imagination', as it is now called (238:36-7), earlier primed by German novels, is now up to composing its own fiction. Eventually a turning point (or peripeteia) is reached, with Lizaveta not only granting Hermann an assignation, but providing exact instructions not only for a nocturnal incursion into the Countess' house, but into her very study-boudoir, although the intention is to inveigle him up to her own attic room, by means of 'a narrow, spiral staircase' (239:12). According to Lotman (1990: 85-6), Lizaveta is here transformed by 'petty egoism' into 'a clockwork doll'.

The ambiance of Hermann's suspenseful wait in the extreme climatic conditions is graphically described, as is his entry to the house, with minute attention to time (' "psychological" time', as it is termed by Seleznev, 1974: 427). The precise description of the habitation has frequently been commented on. Point of view is somewhat indeterminate here; the information seems dispassionate and is narratorially derived, yet the furnishings of the bedroom are said to stand 'in sorrowful symmetry' (239:37), raising the question as to the origin of such an emotion. A cluster of names and artifacts from the eighteenth century are given to add period and appurtenance flavour: Madame Lebrun, the painter of two Parisian portraits hanging therein (which may be presumed to be those of the young Countess and her husband), clocks by Leroy and the (here gratuitous) names of the balloonists Montgolfier and Mesmer the magnetist (that of Galvani soon follows).

Hermann advances beyond the 'screens' (240:6), frequently referred to in the Countess' bedroom and in that of Lizaveta. Instead of taking the door to the left, and the winding staircase up to Lizaveta's room, Hermann takes the one to the right, into the Countess' 'dark boudoir' (240:10, her *kabinet* or inner sanctum), there to await the old lady's return. She eventually arrives and sinks into 'the Voltaire armchair' (240:21). Through a chink from the boudoir, Hermann watches first Lizaveta pass by and then is witness to 'the revolting secrets of [the Countess'] toilet' (240:29). Left alone finally, she sits rocking herself in the Voltaire armchair, as though 'by hidden Galvanism' (240:40), illuminated only by the icon lamp.

Suddenly 'before the Countess there stood an unknown man' (241:2-3). This is, of course, Hermann, who now makes his move to confront the Countess, although the possibility cannot be discounted that the Countess mistakes him for someone else (as Kodjak wishes to believe) – however, it would seem to stretch the text somewhat to read it as though she was expecting someone. Another dialogue with the deaf ensues. Hermann begins to quiz the Countess, but she 'it seemed, did not hear him' (241:7). Nevertheless, as he persists, she 'it seemed understood what was wanted of her; it seemed she was looking for words for her reply' (241:13-14). Finally, she declares: ' – It was a joke, ...I swear to you! it was a joke!' (241:15-16). Whether 'truth' or evasion, this statement is tantamount to a fifth reaction to Tomsky's original anecdote (and yet a further reaction to, or interpretation of, the work as a whole). In no mood to be fobbed off, Hermann tries the name Chaplitsky on her and she is 'visibly embarrassed' (241:19). As he tries to produce arguments as to why he should be entrusted with the three-card secret, Hermann declares that 'he who cannot preserve his father's legacy will in any case die in poverty, notwithstanding any demonic forces' (241:26-7). This amounts to a prophetic statement of his own fate and is another virtual *mise en abyme* utterance (this time for the *fabula* rather than the work as a whole).

Demanding the 'secret' (241:37 and 242:1), Hermann uses every sentimental argument he can muster and then moves on to speculation on a 'devil's bargain' (241:39, thus inspiring the interpretation of Kodjak and others) and makes his own offer to take this upon himself (which perhaps 'did not remain unnoticed *there*' – Seleznev, 1974: 431). Her continuing silence causes him to lose his nerve; he calls her an 'old witch' (242:7), threatens her and produces his ('unloaded', he later says – 245:12-13) pistol. This, not surprisingly, produces a 'strong feeling' in the old woman (242:10-11). Her nodding and raising of the arm ('as though shielding herself from a shot', 242:11-12) may be a sign finally of willingness to comply, or it may be something else. In any event, she apparently expires at that moment. Hermann does not immediately recognise this fact, telling her, with gross inappropriateness, to stop 'playing the child' (*perestan'te rebiachit'sia*, 242:13).

Chapter IV

The even shorter epigraph to Chapter IV, '*7 Mai 18**. Homme sans moeurs et sans religion!*', again ascribed to 'Correspondence', was long thought to have been a Pushkinian invention, like most of the other epigraphs; however, in recent years it has been identified by Gareth Williams (1981: 218) as having been taken from Voltaire's 'Dialogue d'un Parisien et d'un Russe' (1760). On the surface this quotation seems to be a comment on Hermann; however, other Voltairian references and the context may throw up other interpretations and Williams suggests that it is really intended as an allusion to Pushkin's exile and part of a wider polemic against Alexander I, which emerges from hidden meanings of the epigraphs in totality.[11]

Lizaveta has gone up to her room, 'hoping to find there Hermann, and wishing not to find him' (243:9). Discovering his absence, she ruminates on the astonishing developments of the past three weeks and in particular over her mazurka-time conversation with Tomsky at the ball which has just ended: some of his teasing was so accurate that she thought 'her secret was known to him' (243:26-7). There are a number of interesting points in this conversation (reported in direct speech, as though a flashback). Tomsky says he knows what he knows 'from the friend of someone you know, ...a very remarkable man' (243:29-30). The 'remarkable man' is revealed as Hermann; the identity of the 'friend' is not pursued; one would assume Narumov to be the most likely candidate. At this point Tomsky conveys the oft-quoted comment on Hermann that 'he has the profile of Napoleon and the soul of Mephistopheles' (244:2) and that, Tomsky thinks, 'he has at least three crimes on his conscience' (244:3). Drawn out further, Tomsky supposes Hermann himself to have an interest in Lizaveta, declares that 'he very keenly listens to the enamoured exclamations of his friend' (244:9-10) and, most mysteriously (or mischievously), that he 'is capable' of having seen her 'in your room, while you were asleep' (244:13). The conversation is then interrupted, and the narrator, while stressing the effect of these words on Lizaveta, dismisses them as 'nothing more than mazurka chatter' (244:23). Such a figure as Hermann, in Tomsky's depiction, seems familiar to her, 'thanks to the latest novels' (244:26).

Back in the present of the tale, Hermann enters and confesses what has occurred. Tomsky's words then immediately return to Lizaveta's consciousness. She is even more horrified as his confession unfolds; 'Money, that is what his soul craved!' (245:1-2). The only thing which horrified Hermann however, we are told, was 'the irreparable loss of the secret, from which he had expected opulence' (245:9-10). Lizaveta's eventual accusation, 'You are a monster!' (245:11), seems to balance Hermann's hurling of the epithet 'old witch' at the Countess (242:7). In the faint morning light (hours seem to have gone past – see Pursglove, 1985) Hermann seems again to resemble 'surprisingly…a portrait of Napoleon' (245:18-19), this time both to the narrator and to Lizaveta Ivanovna (who would still be remembering Tomsky's words). Lizaveta is nevertheless prepared to expedite Hermann's departure from the Countess' house by a 'secret staircase' (245:21) and allows him to shake her 'cold unresponsive hand' and kiss her 'bent brow' in farewell (245:25-6).

Hermann retraces his steps, looks long at the old woman, who was as though 'turned to stone;[12] her face expressed deep calm' (245:29-30). As he descends the 'dark staircase' towards escape, he is 'agitated by strange feelings' (245:32-3). The dominant one is apparently the idea of a former lover of the Countess creeping along this staircase 'perhaps about sixty years ago', while 'the heart of his ancient mistress has today ceased beating' (245:34 and 38).

Chapter V

The epigraph to Chapter V is in Russian and is attributed to the famed Swedish mystic, Swedenborg. However, its provenance in Swedenborg's prolific writings has never been identified and it is generally held to have been composed by Pushkin (were it not to have been, it would probably not have been quoted in Russian, for a start). Again, it may relate to Pushkin himself and to Alexander I's mystical propensities (see Williams, 1981: 219-22). Its relevance to Chapter V of *The Queen of Spades* is again ironical and oblique ('That night the late Baroness von V*** appeared to me. She was all in white and she said to me: "How do you do, Mr. Councillor!" '). The supposed apparition of the Countess is clad in white; if we ignore the 'Mr. Councillor' form of address (which may just be intended to relate to Swedenborg), we are left with perhaps a typically sceptical Pushkinian aside on the not infrequent tendency on the part of revenants to have nothing of consequence to impart if and when they do return. This may, or may not, influence our inclination to take seriously either the posthumous appearance of the Countess or the message she brings.

Three days later, Hermann attends the funeral of the Countess, though not exactly from remorse. His conscience suggests: 'you are the murderer of the old woman!' (246:10) and, rather like Pushkin himself, he is said to be stronger on superstition than on faith; her potentially 'harmful influence on his life' and the possibility of obtaining her 'forgiveness' (246:12-14) are on his mind. Amid a church crowded with society associates, servants and three generations of family, a 'young bishop' (246:24) makes the funeral address (the youth of such a bishop seems to demand explanation: none has been offered, although Pursglove, 1985:15-16, has drawn attention to youth and age as a theme in the work).[13] The references to 'the righteous' (246:25-6), her 'Christian end' (246:27), the 'angel of death' and 'awaiting the midnight bridegroom' (246:27-9) (the last constituting an allusion to the parable of the wise and foolish virgins, from Matthew 25: 1-13) all strike an ironical note, given the details as we know them of the Countess' life and of her death, and perhaps stand in counterpoint to (the presumed wise virgin) Lizaveta's 'tallow candle darkly burning in a brass candlestick' (234:21).

The funeral scene has been described by Heidi Faletti (1977: 127) as 'replete with grotesque happenings anticipating [Hermann's] ultimate downfall' and at the same time 'an uncanny link between the world of routine reality and supernatural forces'. Point of view switches from the narrator to Hermann, as the dead Countess, 'it seemed to him…screwed up one eye' (247:7-8) and back again. Hermann, stepping back, 'crashed to the ground *on his back*' (247:9-10; my emphasis). It is not expressly said that he hit his head on the hard church floor but, if he did, the consequences could be far reaching. Lizaveta Ivanovna is carried out 'in a swoon' (247:11) at the same moment.

In the minor confusion which follows, 'a lean chamberlain' (whom Williams [1981:211-12] endeavours to identify at some level as Voltaire), said to be 'a close relative of the deceased' (247:13-14), but one we have not met or heard of before (as far as we know), whispers to (for some reason) an Englishman (not as yet identified by anyone!) that 'the young officer is her illegitimate son' (247:15). This is clearly nonsense, for any number of reasons, but has a certain spiritual resonance, as well as providing a pretext for some critics to seek, and find, alternative illegitimate sons elsewhere in the tale. Like the epigraphs, this assertion seems to have at best an oblique relevance, a kind of negative inappropriateness, although significance at some level cannot be excluded.

We then pass, in just two brief paragraphs, from funeral to apparition. Hermann's wining and dining are frequently read as exposing him to inebriated hallucination; a close reading can equally provide grounds for an opposing plea. The time at which he awakes is seen as closely corresponding to the time of the Countess's demise (Pursglove, 1985: 18 n.6). The other circumstances of the 'visitation' – the locked door, the shuffling shoes, the mistaking of the woman in white by Hermann for his 'old nurse' (247:31-2), the symmetrical peerings in at the window – only serve to heighten the mystification and clearly can be read in more than one way (see for instance Kodjak, 1976: 102-3, who stresses the narrator's function as 'eyewitness'; Cornwell, 1990: 119).

Passing from the purported messenger to the message, we find that just about everything to do with it is significant. The fact that the revenant came to Hermann 'against my will' (247:35) would, were it taken seriously (as it is by Kodjak), suggest an otherworld cabal with its own hierarchy to be in operation. Like the Countess in Paris (according to the anecdote), Hermann is given the names of three cards (on this occasion at least, 'the three, the seven and the ace' [247:36-7]) to play in order; like Chaplitsky he is forbidden to play again for life; unlike either of the previous two, so far as we know, he can only play his cards at the rate of one a day (possibly, in the view of Rosen, 1975: 257, to increase the suspense). The Countess and Chaplitsky seem to have played their three cards one after the other. The rules seem to get clearer each time we hear of them; they also seem to alter, evolve, or become stricter (noted too by Labriolle, 1969: 264; and by Pike). Hermann at least had his capital to put on the his first card; the Countess and Chaplitsky were allegedly able to win with no money to stake in the first place (also noted by Labriolle: 264-5). And, this time, that is not all. The apparition declares that she will forgive Hermann her death on condition that he marry her ward, Lizaveta Ivanovna. The goalposts move as the rules evolve, as the secrets and the plotlines intertwine.

Chapter VI

The epigraph to Chapter VI is again in Russian (apart from the word *attendez* in French) and is this time unattributed.[14] It obviously derives from the milieu of gambling; the point of the original centres on the use of the enclitic '*s*' in pre-revolutionary Russian: a mark of subordination or of cringing respect (the nearest equivalent being 'sir'). The use of such an enclitic with a French word (*attendez*, already in the formal form; here a gambling term, indicating to the banker that a punter wishes to make or change a bet) is in itself semi-farcical. It illustrates the Russian nobility's mixed linguistic nature in society and the potentially carnivalised situation of the gaming room, in which the relatively low-classes may momentarily equal the rich and the great. More specifically, in the context of the finale of *The Queen of Spades*, the suggestion is that someone may be speaking or acting above his station. One commentator (Shvartsband, 1988: 150-1) seems to think the epigraph is a statement made by the banker to the punter (by Chekalinsky, in other words, to Hermann).

Chapter VI opens with Hermann's obsession with the 'three, seven, ace' formula; this dominated his thoughts when awake and 'pursued him in sleep' (249:14-15). The narrator claims that 'two fixed ideas' cannot coexist simultaneously (249:6). If the dominant idea is that of the formula, another idea must have been subjugated; this, one would presume, must be the idea of forgiveness for the death of the Countess, bound up under the conditions imposed with marriage to Lizaveta Ivanovna. This particular neglect may well have serious consequences.

The imagery of Hermann's daydreaming (*mechta*) and nocturnal dreaming (*son*) has led to considerable critical speculation. In the latter, the three becomes like 'a magnificent magnolia', the seven 'Gothic gates' and the ace 'a huge spider' (249:15-17). Nathan Rosen reproduces photographs of actual Russian playing cards of the period (partly reprinted here as Fig. 3) and convincingly argues their relevance to the dream imagery (Rosen, 1975: 262-4). Visual and sonic associations link the three of hearts with a slender girl (249:11-12), the seven with the time ('five minutes to the seven', 249:13) and the ace 'a pot-bellied man' (249:13). Amid the transformations of dream, the three (girl) becomes a grandiloquent flower; the seven (time) can be seen to resemble a Gothic portal (see Rosen, 1975: 264); and the ace (*tuz*, rich man) metamorphoses into a big (and destructive?) spider (the spider might even encompass both ace and queen, ibid.: 266). The cards of 1830 had right-angled corners and no mark in the upper left hand corner. The three (girl and flower) are seen as positive signs (ibid.: 264); not so the seven and the ace. The Gothic seven represents the dark side of the tale, back in time, and its Gothic elements; a spider is not unlike the ace of spades in shape and, if magnified, not so unlike the queen. The story itself, *Pikovaia dama*: the 'spade lady', becomes *paukovaia dama*: the 'spider lady' (ibid.: 266-7), in both sound and vision. Equally, perhaps, Hermann himself could be seen here emblematically as a spider, caught in the framework of a Gothic tale.

'Is the girl the Countess (as seen in her portrait) or Lizaveta?' asks Rosen (p. 263), preferring to settle for the latter. The identification which Rosen does not make, however, is that between the queen of spades, as she appears on the card of that period, and the young Countess, as described in relation to what is presumed to be her portrait ('a young beauty with an aquiline nose, hair brushed back at the temples and a rose in her powdered hair', 239:40-240:2); in the case of the queen, the rose is in her hand (this likeness has been noted, however, by Williams, 1983: 391-2). Rosen proceeds by referring to similarities between the queen framed as a card; the Countess framed against the (high) back of her Voltaire chair and by her rectangular coffin; and someone's head (twice) framed by the window on the occasion of the ghostly visitation to Hermann (Rosen, 1975: 268). All are seen as preparatory to the final identification of the queen with the old Countess ('The old woman!', 251:40).

So much for the first paragraph of Chapter VI. Indeed, we have not quite done yet with the first paragraph. Hermann can think of nothing but exploiting the three-card secret, perhaps in Paris, when 'chance' intervenes, we are told (249:20), in the form of a visit to St Petersburg of the noted Moscow gambler Chekalinsky. It is Narumov who conducts Hermann to Chekalinsky's gambling den. Chekalinsky is 'a man of about sixty, of most respectable appearance' (250:2-3); the latter phrase echoes exactly the description of Saint-Germain in Chapter I (228:38) and, although most descriptions put him a bit younger looking (see Appendix), Saint-Germain would have been thought to have been about sixty in 1770. This similarity may or may not be coincidental. Narumov, we may notice, congratulates Hermann on 'the breaking of a long-lasting fast' (250:17-18) as he begins to play and wishes him 'beginner's luck'.

This is exactly what Hermann seems to possess, as his first card, for the unusually large sum of 47,000 roubles, wins: the three. Narumov is flabbergasted, while Hermann drinks a glass of lemonade (251:9). The narrative resumes only at the same time the next day (and then subsequently on the third day). Hermann bets the same sum, plus the day before's winnings, and again wins: with the seven. Hermann takes his 94,000 'with composure' (251:19). On the third evening his arrival is awaited by a lively crowd of officers and civil servants. Chekalinsky is 'pale, but still smiling' (251:26): 'It was like a duel' (251:29). Hermann thinks he has won, saying 'the ace has won!' (251:33) but, revealing his card, soon finds otherwise: ' – Your queen is beaten, – said Chekalinsky gently' (251:34). Gently or otherwise, what Chekalinsky actually says is ambiguous in Russian and could equally translate as 'your lady has been killed'.[15] Hermann is actually in possession, whatever the explanation for this may be, of the queen of spades and not the winning ace (which actually does, or would, win – but for the bank: see the diagrammatic representation of the three games in Fig. 1). Such a statement from Chekalinsky hardly restores his equanimity, a mocking wink seems to emanate from the (albeit young!) queen on the card and the horrified identification with 'the old woman!' is completed (251:40). A rather strange 'excellently punted!' is exclaimed (252:3), but it is not clear to whom this is addressed. 'The game resumed its normal course' (252:4) is the closing statement of the tale proper. It is thus framed by an opening and a closing of nocturnal winter card-play in St Petersburg.

The 'Conclusion' (of three short paragraphs totalling just eight lines) is appended almost as an epilogue, a traditional ending by which the reader is aquainted with the subsequent fortunes of the main characters of a fictional work. It deals with the fates of three characters: that of Hermann – madness; that of Lizaveta Ivanovna – marriage, wealth and the upbringing of a poor (female) relation of her own; and that of Tomsky (here included for reasons that are unclear) – promotion and marriage. The implications of the Conclusion have been discussed at some length by Shaw (1962) and others. Hermann's mutterings of 'Three, seven ace! Three, seven, queen!' show clearly that he remains obsessed with the three-card formula and its catastrophic variant. Whether his preoccupation at this stage is with the game of faro, lost wealth, or (as Barker, 1984: 208, believes) the old woman is a moot point (just one among others).

Readings of
The Queen of Spades

The foregoing Commentary is designed as a reading aid and not as an interpretative reading *per se*. A discussion of what is involved in producing the latter is what remains to be undertaken.

It may cause little surprise that the Commentary left, or indicated, a number of loose ends. For a start, a number of key words or concepts seem to obtrude from the text (and from many commentaries on it): the word 'secret' (in terms of number, nature and authenticity); the rules of the game (or games: who is playing whom or what and in which or whose game?); the word 'joke' and its possible resonance. The role of minor characters has attracted attention in certain quarters and will inevitably arise again below. Other controversial points have been discussed, if not resolved, to a greater or lesser extent: the epigraphs; the seeming oddity of Tomsky being a 'prince'; the imagery of Hermann's dreams – not that the last word has been uttered, in all probability, on these or many other matters.

Before going on to categorise readings or interpretations of *The Queen of Spades*, there are a number of previously suggested schemes of approach which we may care to consider or to note. Ann Shukman (1977: 69-70) divides the work into two plotlines (that of Hermann and that of Lizaveta Ivanovna) and the overall plot into two sections (the events which take place up to the death of the old Countess and those thereafter). Within this scheme, three peripeteias (or turning points) are identified. Two occur within Hermann's plotline and form virtual mirror images of each other: Hermann comes to the Countess and as a result loses all hope; the (ghostly) Countess comes to Hermann and restores hope. The third peripeteia is within Lizaveta Ivanovna's plotline: Hermann's confession that he was only interested in her as a means to the old woman's secret destroys her own 'secret', her hopes in him as a deliverer. Such a scheme of structural analysis, followed through more fully, can lead (as we shall see), but not necessarily, to something like a fairy tale reading.

Somewhat similar results may come from a consideration of 'three worlds', drawn by Roberta Reeder (1982: 95) by analogy with Hoffmann. These comprise the philistine world devoid of the irrational (in which Tomsky and friends live); a fantasy/make-believe world of dreams of fortune and sentimental love (to which both Hermann and Lizaveta Ivanovna may seem to belong); and a demonic realm of Mephistophelian dominion (of which the Countess and Saint-Germain are likely denizens).

This may remind us of, and we may prefer to return to, the scheme suggested by the three initial lines of response to Tomsky's anecdote: this would provide a world of chance or fate (in which explanations are otherwise at least nominally rational); a world of fairy tale (in which one may, or may not, believe); and a world of sharp practice, governed by malignant hoaxers. There is enough breadth here to cover most interpretations, the more so if we recall and add in the possibilities inherent in the fourth response (that of 'cabalistics') and the belated fifth ('a joke'), as well as focusing on ambiguities previously noted within the first three.

Three main groups of interpretation are identified by Doherty (1992: 50): those with a mainly literary-historical or textological concern; those attempting a formal or structural analysis of the text; and those attempting an 'exegesis' of the text, 'revealing some hidden, often occult, meaning'. Emerson (1992: 23) formulates four categories of approach. Her first is that of 'socio-literary studies that focus on the mechanics and ideology behind gambling' (Lotman: 1975 and Rosen: 1975, for all their differences, are quoted as examples). Secondly comes the 'psychoanalytical–generational treatments' (here Schwartz and Schwartz: 1975 and Burgin: 1974 – again for all their differences – are the exemplars). Thirdly she cites 'linguistic and syntactic studies' (of which Vinogradov: 1980 – originally 1936 and 1941 – is the founder; and Faletti: 1977 a more recent instance). The fourth category named is that of the numerological study (exemplified naturally by the essays of Leighton).

In some ways analogous, and certainly in tune with the 'readerly' approach overall of both Doherty and Emerson – two of the most recent commentators on *The Queen of Spades* – is C.R. Pike's disposition of the 'concentric circles' of the story's readership: the innermost circle is seen as Pushkin's own friends and circle (some of whom had even contributed anecdotal elements); secondly come the echelons of aristocracy and Court (whose reaction Pushkin had cautiously to note); and then the outer circle, that of the reading public of the day, 'the nascent intelligentsia' (Pike: unpublished).

None of these categoric schemes seems to account comprehensively for the range of readings that we have observed, although it is perhaps no accident that the one based on the responses to Tomsky's anecdote may come the closest (if seen as a *mise en abyme* for the entire tale and the process of reading it). If we have established anything in this study so far, it must be that not only have a plurality of readings been offered of *The Queen of Spades* but that there would appear to be elements within the story which seem likely to support multiple readings. Regardless at this stage of whether we may wish to fix ultimately on any single reading, we may begin by considering some guidelines as to what might constitute a 'good' or a 'bad' (or terms to that effect: 'strong' or 'weak', 'full' or 'partial') reading. A 'good' ('strong' or 'full') reading should answer all, or as many as possible, of the questions raised by the text in a satisfactory manner, as may be demonstrated by reference to the text. 'Bad' readings may fail to do this, or only manage to accomplish this result by illegitimate means. 'Partial' readings may well partly satisfy their readership (hypothetically a wide readership of *The Queen of Spades* and, in theory at least, its Russian readership, as well as that comprising western Russianists and their students, or general readers who approach the text in translation), but they either deal with only some of the issues arising from the story or leave questions unanswered. Even if we should find there to be more than one 'good' or 'strong' reading, we may still prefer one to another on the grounds of the overall impact on the work of accepting a particular reading. Both Rosen (1975: 259) and Mersereau (1989), for instance, reject the interpretation that the Countess deliberately deceived and destroyed Hermann, on the grounds that 'if this is correct the psychological significance of the story is vitiated and Pushkin is deprived of his proper claim to have introduced a significant theme into Russian fiction' (Mersereau, 1989: 177).

Perhaps we should at least briefly look at, if only then to discard, some 'bad', 'weak' or 'partial' readings, before proceeding to a consideration of some of what we might take to be the 'stronger' ones.

Some of these we have already commented on in our Part One survey. Historical readings, for example, for all their potential interest in terms of research and detail, must be dubious if they mix, and indeed confuse, the roles of fictional characters (such as the Countess) and historical prototypes (such as Princess Golitsyna). There is no need here to go any further in attempting to distinguish between the historical, the mythological and the fictional versions of Saint-Germain (see on this the Appendix). Redating the setting of the story (or of the anecdote) in order to accommodate supposed Decembrist or other political allusions may be superficially attractive, but appears to have little basis even outside the text, let alone within it. The presence in the text for instance of gematria as identified by Leighton (1977B) is another matter and must be indicative of something; but, as with numerological readings, this seems to have been a quality which has been implanted in the work, but it can scarcely be considered to be its primary purpose. If Pushkin did leave pro-Decembrist messages encoded here and there in his texts, that is not to say that he equated this penchant in itself with the true function of art.

'Bad' readings must also include those which depend on unsubstantiated information from beyond the text: on this occasion perhaps not

from historical or Pushkinian sources, but merely from putting together
veiled hints and allusions from the text and leaping to unwarranted conclusions. We have seen quite a number of instances of this sort of argument in
our critical survey, centering mostly on claims made regarding amorous
intrigues of the past and involving the Countess (with Saint-Germain and/or
Chaplitsky). While the general tone of the narrative, within the main text and
especially the anecdote, might suggest the probability that assumptions as to
amorous escapades in general may be justified, there would appear to be no
hard evidence to establish any facts in any particular case; indeed, the quip
as to Hermann being the Countess' illegitimate son (which is impossible if
only for the vast difference in their ages) seems in itself to signal caution.
The sparse narrative of *The Queen of Spades*, the general sense felt by all
readers of selectivity and the withholding of vital information, of course,
have fuelled such speculative, almost criminological, readings. As with the
quality of the supernatural, however, once admitted, extra-textual 'facts'
know no bounds. We shall return to this topic again when examining the
possibilities for a hoax theory.

Legitimate, though perhaps limited, is a category which has been identified as the numerological reading. At times the research which has gone into
such readings and the ingenuity of the researcher can be impressive, verging
on the mind-boggling. These findings also demonstrably exist within the text
(Leighton's articles indeed are textual readings *par excellence*). Nevertheless, they seem to me to qualify as only partial, or limited, readings: firstly
because of their concentration on a single aspect (numerological or lexical
formations with or without a hidden message); and secondly because, given
even that such findings may be correct (and in fact it is often indisputable
that they are), it is still difficult to believe that this represents Pushkin's only,
or even primary, intention. Leighton himself is ready to admit this: for
Pushkin, 'gematria was one more practice – together with numerology,
cartomancy, covert allusions' and so on – 'by which to make "The Queen of
Spades" one of the most intriguing works in all world literature'; while, as
for Freemasonry, even when 'fully revealed, it is by no means clear how
seriously it is to be taken' (Leighton, 1982: 22-3). For Felix Raskolnikoff too
(1987: 259), the 'magic of numbers' is there to serve the aim of the creation
of a 'fantastic backdrop' and is not needed for literal reading.

Also under the label of partial or weak readings, we can include many
examples of psychological readings. These can be seen to fall into two sub-
categories. The first is anxious to impose a psychological interpretation on
the tale, usually in order to confirm realism (rather than the Gothic or
romanticism) as Pushkin's guiding compositional principle. Traditional Soviet criticism has been particularly active in this regard, but, as we have seen,
a number of western critics have chosen to pursue the same line. The second
sub-category has been to attempt a psychoanalytical reading of the work, on

the basis of a number of ingredients within the text (for instance, the attraction apparently felt by Hermann for the Countess as a mother figure and the possessor of a mysterious power). The latter case has yet to be argued as satisfactorily as it might. The former invariably leaves itself open to charges of failing to answer, or even to pay any attention to, key events in the plot (*siuzhet*), such as Hermann's winning cards. We shall return to the prospects for both brands of psychological reading below.

A further tendency which has developed has been to read *The Queen of Spades* through a subsequent fictional work, itself said to have been inspired by, or to depend for its existence wholly or in part upon, *The Queen of Spades*. Such a reverse reading, unless centred mainly on the later work (in which case source spotting or intertextuality becomes the name of the game), must also be a partial reading, concentrating on elements which have been reproduced or reworked elsewhere. A number of Soviet studies, as we have seen, have been interested in links between *The Queen of Spades* and Dostoevsky's *Crime and Punishment*. A small group of western commentators (to one of whom, Carlos Fuentes, we shall return in search of further development) have established Pushkin's tale as a prototypical text for Henry James.[16] However, intertextual studies of this type are beyond our current remit.

Let us return to the initial three responses given to Tomsky's anecdote ('chance', 'fairy tale' and 'hoax') as a range of possible interpretations of the overall work. We may now find that what we have considered to be the two supplementary answers ('cabalistics' and 'a joke') can be accommodated within the original three after all. First 'chance' (*sluchai*). This, it has been suggested, may be subdivided into 'pure chance' or the heavy hand of fate. Pure chance is the only answer offered by psychological-realist critics hitherto to the phenomenon of Hermann's winning cards; many commentators, as we have seen, find this unacceptable, indeed harder to believe than the apparent alternative of the supernatural. I shall attempt to indicate, later below, a psychological reading which does not leave itself open to this objection. The idea of the hand of fate seems to gell suitably with Pushkin's known propensity for superstition; however, in itself it comprises a sort of unexplained (and inexplicable: the hand of fate is both heavy and hidden) version of the supernatural and leaves open the question of apparently overt supernatural interventions within the tale.

'Fairy tale' (*skazka*) also subdivides: into the metaphorical and the literal; even the literal (magical) meaning can perhaps be further subdivided. The metaphorical reading of fairy tale would suggest story-telling, in the sense of a possibly charming but essentially untrue anecdote. If the original (Tomsky's) anecdote is make-believe, then the rest of *The Queen of Spades* is built on 'misreading', or gross misinterpretation on Hermann's part (but, still, what of his winning cards?). This might then conform to the Countess' proffered explanation ('a joke'), to the idea of fairy tale as 'nonsense', and to Pushkin's overall intention of composing a literary joke, or general parody, with the popular Hoffmannian (plus Gothic and French freneticist) tale as his 'architext'.[17] This is certainly one possible interpretation of *The Queen of Spades* and is close to the conclusions that have been advanced by a number of critics. In the present age of reader-consciousness it may have a certain appeal.

If we take a more magical, and therefore literal, interpretation of fairy tale, we can arrive at the type of Proppian fairy (or folk) tale reading of *The Queen of Spades* which has been favoured by Ann Shukman (1977: 69-70) and others.[18] This may be stated as follows in tabulated form of main, or representative, plot functions (or elements):

1. Tomsky tells anecdote of grandmother's secret.
2. Countess had intrigued with Saint-Germain sixty years before and received the secret of the three cards and won.
3. Chaplitsky, who might or might not have been the illegitimate son of the Countess and Saint-Germain, is given the secret and also wins.
4. Hermann appears outside the Countess' house.
5. Lizaveta receives and eventually submits to approaches by Hermann.
6. Hermann clumsily tackles the Countess over her secret (his Mistake No. 1).
7. Countess says secret was a 'joke'.
8. Countess nods, raises her arm and immediately dies of shock.
9. Tomsky has told Lizaveta things about Hermann.
10. Hermann confesses all to Lizaveta and leaves Countess' house.
11. Priest's officiation at Countess' funeral.
12. Dead Countess seems to wink at Hermann.
13. Countess' ghost appears, imparts secret and instructs Hermann to marry Lizaveta.
14. Idea of winning drives guilt and marriage from Hermann's mind (his Mistake No. 2).
15. (Protracted) confrontation with Chekalinsky: Hermann loses, turning up queen of spades (seen by him as Countess).
16. Epilogue: Hermann has gone mad, Lizaveta has found a husband.

The self-evident proximity of the plotlines of *The Queen of Spades* to the fairy tale has been noted by Shukman (1977: 76-7) who gives the following summary of the archetype:

The classic Russian fairy tale had as its core the story of the hero who is despatched, journeys to another kingdom, acquires a magic object, overcomes the antagonist, wins the princess.... A standard theme of the fairy tales...is that the hero, to achieve his aim, must receive from the donor the magic object. The donor, a distinct functionary in Propp's list, is an ambivalent figure who may assist or not, who imposes certain conditions, or tests, on the hero.

Hermann as questing hero, the formula (of the three cards) as the passport to riches – the prize, along with Lizaveta, the 'princess' – and the Countess as donor are obvious as fairy-tale elements. Mistakes made, however, or tests failed, lead to disaster against the final antagonist (here Chekalinsky). Hermann's overall mistake, in terms of the classic fairy tale, is that, instead of striving to win fortune and bride, he misuses the latter in his single-minded attempt to gain the former. Shukman herself, however, points out that such a reading of the story is 'to assume the actual involvement of the spirit of the dead Countess' (ibid. 77) – 'an unambiguous interpretation' which, strictly speaking, neither she nor I would wish to admit. However, we cannot have fairy tale without at least an element of magic. Moreover, the using of 'love' to gain riches, while 'a reversal of the folktale stereotype', was of course to become 'one of the leading subjects of nineteenth-century literature' (ibid.).

If a fairy-tale reading of *The Queen of Spades* involves the acceptance of one kind of supernatural, a pervasive atmosphere of 'faerie', so does any reading which interprets '*skazka*' as a deeper magic. This could bring us to something of the order of a 'cabalistic' reading, involving a conspiracy of occult forces, and result in an interpretation akin to that of Kodjak (1976). Here, of course, we encounter once again familiar objections to do with the illimitability of the supernatural, once admitted, and the dangers of making assumptions outside the text (which, if the supernatural is permitted, seem somehow that much more allowable).

And now, what of the hoax? One may fairly assume that, were such a device to be at the bottom of *The Queen of Spades*, it would have to comprise something more than mere malpractice over either a single hand or a series of card games (although an element of this might at some stage be involved). We have frequently remarked on the perceived presence of irony in Pushkin's tale (Maxim Shrayer: 1992 has recently re-stressed this in terms of romantic irony). We have also noted the sparcity of information and detail provided in the tale, in terms of narrative selectivity and the withholding of knowledge. Furthermore, after the manner in which Schlegel approached irony, we may care to note that 'everything one believes is both true and false' (Shrayer, 1992: 397). Tomsky, as we have seen, dismisses the 'marked cards' suggestion as an explanation of his original anecdote; however, as already remarked, his word may not be conclusive: if there is any element of fraud or conspiracy, it is a fair bet that Tomsky must be involved therein. Žekulin (1987: 79) asks a number of questions about Tomsky and sees him as a 'temptor'. Delbert Phillips (1982: 102) suggests, in respect of the ghostly visitation, that 'Herman's officer friends may be playing a trick on him', while 'perhaps the ghost is the old countess's feeble housekeeper forced against her will to participate in a charade'. By 'housekeeper' Phillips means the 'old gentlewoman' (*staraia barskaia dama*), of the same age as the Countess, who is the last of the household to bid farewell to her mistress (*gospozha*) at the Countess' funeral. This appears to be the nearest that criticism has come to positing a hoax theory.

That a fully-blown hoax explanation has not been elaborated is scarcely surprising. The paucity of information is such that it is difficult to imagine any such theory standing up to scrutiny without considerable reliance upon data from beyond the text. However, the introduction of such material, in greater or lesser measure, has not of course been eschewed by the proponents of other types of reading. In view of what we have said already, of the 'badness' (or 'weakness') of readings relying on such dubious tactics, let us not take any such reading too seriously; nevertheless, it might be intriguing to follow such a reading further, using only personages who are at least mentioned at some stage in the text (and even providing a tongue-in-cheek explanation in some cases for their otherwise unexplained presence).

A brief outline might go like this. Let us suppose Lizaveta Ivanovna to be the illegitimate daughter of a member of the Countess' family. (Such were frequently brought up as 'poor relatives'-cum-companions and 'Ivanovna' is the likely patronymic for an illegitimate child.) Her father could have been one of the Countess' four (or more) sons: perhaps (but not necessarily) the 'lean chamberlain' who made the crack about Hermann being the illegitimate son of the Countess at the funeral (he is described as a 'near relative' and may be presumed to know of the Countess' actual illegitimate offspring, such as Chekalinsky who, let us say, is the fruit of his mother's old amour with the Count Saint-Germain). We will assume that all that happened up until the death of the Countess is narrated fully enough in the text as we have it. In other words, Hermann became obsessed by the old family anecdote jokingly related by Tomsky and sought access to the Countess by means of a feigned courtship of Lizaveta Ivanovna. Hermann bungled his interview with the Countess and frightened her to death. He confessed his errors to Lizaveta, throwing himself upon her mercy. Here perhaps Pushkin is less than frank with us; despite Lizaveta's initial revulsion, the long night they spent together (from three until the late Petersburg winter dawn) took a natural course and they became lovers. Evidence? Little enough, except the candle images associated with Lizaveta (234:21 and 245:15), which are counterpointed by the removal of the candles from the Countess (240:35): it is Lizaveta, in her *décolletage*, who was awaiting the 'midnight bridegroom' (246:28-9; in the words of the young bishop which have, as usual in this tale, a misleadingly oblique relevance), not the Countess. Such an outcome would also explain the buoyant mood of Hermann's departure down the secret staircase on leaving the house: surely the mood of a man temporarily gloating over amorous conquest, rather than shattered by the loss of any prospect of a fortune.

At this point, we would have to go even further into conjecture. Lizaveta, by now a Karamzinian 'Poor Liza', overcome with remorse, must have confessed all to certain members of the/her family – to Tomsky, at least (who may well be her natural cousin, if not her brother). Anxious to protect Lizaveta's interests and ensure that Hermann does the decent thing, Tomsky, in cahoots with Narumov (an admirer of Lizaveta's, as we already suspect, who must have met her at the Countess' ball [noted by Shvartsband, 1988: 170] and who withdraws his suit at this point), organises the 'old gentlewoman' (as Phillips surmises) to dress in white, impersonating the Countess as dressed in her coffin, to deliver the message from beyond. The 'three, seven, ace' sequence may correspond to the detail of the old family anecdote. Tomsky, who is not mentioned as attending the funeral, may have gone to Moscow to fetch Chekalinsky and set up the *dénouement*. Chekalinsky, who is described as aged about sixty and of the same appearance as Saint-Germain, may be the Countess' son by that liaison. He would therefore be related to, and could even be the father of, Lizaveta Ivanovna. Narumov leads the by now again faro-obsessed Hermann into the lion's den. Chekalinsky has him at his mercy. If he approves of him, and believes he will stand by Lizaveta, he can allow the old 'three-seven-ace' formula to win Hermann a fortune (irrespective of what may have happened in the famous card games of yore); if not, or if fate prompts Hermann to fluff his big chance, the reverse can occur. This, one way or the other is what happens; 'excellently punted!' someone exclaims (perhaps the lean chamberlain). Hermann goes mad and is certified. Lizaveta Ivanovna, having lost both Hermann and Narumov, accepts a proposal, we are told, from the well-to-do son of the Countess' former steward (who no doubt had lined his pockets at her expense); by the 'present' of the tale (1833), she is bringing up a 'poor relative': her own illegitimate daughter by Hermann. Tomsky, the grand orchestrator of these events, will marry his Princess Polina.

Such a reading is of course virtually nonsensical at a primary level and should be ignored by students! Despite any temptations it may hold, it breaks the rules by using material (not pure invention, but creative interpretation, based on persons, hints and non-sequiturs from within the text) from beyond the text, deemed to have been merely 'omitted' by the narrator.

Having thus paid due attention to a number of possible readings of *The Queen of Spades* which may hold superficial attractions, but which nevertheless leave basic questions unresolved and/or many readers sceptical, or which employ dubiously legitimate means such as going beyond the text (pure chance; the supernatural reading; the fairy-tale reading; the joke reading or hoax theory), let us finally outline a selection of what might be more justifiably considered 'stronger' readings. It is particularly to be noted that we are still talking in terms of a plurality and no suggestion is here intended of supplying the last word.

We shall, therefore, revive the fantastic reading (first signalled by Dostoevsky). Then we shall attempt to sketch two distinct psychological readings; and lastly venture two somewhat more speculative interpretations. Many of the arguments surrounding a fantastic, or ambiguous, explication of Pushkin's tale have already been rehearsed at various points of this study (and the case has earlier been argued by me elsewhere: see Cornwell, 1990). It therefore requires only brief recapitulation here.

The question of the fantastic in *The Queen of Spades*, or perhaps rather the issue of supernatural involvement (some element of which must at least have to be considered for serious hesitation on the part of the reader to arise),[19] is normally in this work associated with two things: the secret of the three cards (from Tomsky's anecdote to Hermann's games) and the ghostly visitation of the Countess to Hermann. As we have already seen, the concepts of ambiguity and duality seem to be ingrained in the text at a multiplicity of levels. Many commentators also stress the pervasive presence of the 'mysterious force' and the residual power of a (probably malignant) fate. Plenty has already been said here about Tomsky and his anecdote. Of the Countess, the alleged original recipient of the secret of the cards, it can at least be said that she does appear to know what Hermann is talking about when he demands the secret; however, her only reply, twice uttered, that it was a 'joke' hardly seems, of itself, conclusive confirmation of the veracity of either Tomsky or his anecdote.

The secret of the three cards is directly linked with the ghostly visitation, in that it is this spectral visit which furnishes Hermann with his acquisition of the arcane formula. As we have seen, the issue of Hermann's drunken state at the time is open to interpretation, while we know also that the figures three and seven (and possibly also the ace or one) seemed to be present already in Hermann's mind. These pointers to a psychological reading, however, still leave the usual hoary old questions unresolved. Even if Hermann may have subconsciously intuited, or fixed upon, the values and even the sequence of the three cards, how does he know to play the cards on three separate days? As we have noted, the rules seem to have evolved each time. Even more importantly, if Hermann hallucinated or imagined the formula, how is it that he won on the first two occasions (and indeed that 'three-seven-ace' was in fact – or potentially, at least – the winning sequence in the end)? Marked (or 'powdered') cards? Difficult: new decks were unsealed for each occasion.

The tersely narrated events of the ghostly visitation appear all the more ambiguous the more closely they are looked at (see the comments of Kodjak,

1976: 102). Does the double perspective of the narrator's apparent witness-ing of the visitation confirm the objectivity, or 'reality', of the incident? Even if the incident is 'real', is the visitor necessarily a ghost? Doors opening and banging, the escorting face appearing at the window, the shuffling of the slippers: all of these leave room for doubting the supernatural as it is usually portrayed. Hermann does after all mistake the ghostly figure at first for 'his old wet nurse'. However, we have already looked at the difficulties involved in mounting a convincing hoax theory from the paucity of detail provided by the text. It seems clear that Pushkin does not provide answers to these and other questions; at vital moments the Pushkinian narrator will insist on using phrases such as 'probably' and 'it seemed to him', which potentially leave the event open to either an irrational or a realistic reading. If Pushkin has deliberately constructed a work with such artifice as to ensure that no definitive answers may be given, it would seem perfectly justifiable to argue that the tale remains within the realm of the pure fantastic: the reader cannot decide either way and any attempt to do so will be beset with valid objections.

However, not all critics and readers regard the question of the presence or otherwise of the supernatural in the story as crucial; or else they are prepared to accept its possible presence simply as part of the story and to place the real emphasis elsewhere. If the work is regarded as essentially an amalgam of devices, a parody, or a non-interpretable literary joke, then any inquiry into the 'real' circumstances of events is ultimately 'irrelevant' (as suggested by Debreczeny, 1983: 200). Alternatively, the main emphasis may be seen to fall upon the psychological aspects of the tale. As we have already seen, a distinction may be made between psychological and psychoanalytical readings.

Let us take the former first. A psychological reading – in other words a 'realistic' interpretation of the tale – normally depends upon claims of hallucination: Tomsky's anecdote is just a joke, or pure nonsense; Hermann hallucinates the Countess' wink, the ghostly visitation and the apparent transformation of the queen of spades into the image of the Countess. The stumbling block in such readings, as a rule, is that they offer no explanation, other perhaps than one of pure chance, for the 'three-seven-ace' formula turning out to be a winner. The only way round this problem would seem to require some means whereby the card games with Chekalinsky could be included within the portion of the action deemed to be hallucinated. Strangely enough, I cannot find a critical reading which has attempted to put this argument.

A number of commentators have taken at least a step down this path by volunteering answers to the question: when did Hermann (begin to) go mad? The traditional answer would be that this occurred as a result of the disaster of his third round with Chekalinsky and the resultant loss of his original (patrimonial) capital. However, there may be other possible answers. Mako-gonenko (1982: 254) considers that Hermann was already in a state of delirium (*bred*) by the start of Chapter VI, which turns into a pathological madness after his ultimate loss. If Hermann indeed hallucinated the visitation of the Countess, then this might have been due either to a temporary (inebriated) state or to a more permanently disturbed one. Žekulin (1987: 74) also thinks that the imagery at the beginning of the final chapter shows that 'obsession' has turned into 'madness'. Some others put the onset of Hermann's mental condition at an earlier stage. Shvartsband (1988: 173-4) sees evidence of Hermann's already sickening mind in his jaunty thoughts as he leaves the Countess' house; Lerner (1929: 144 n.1) had reached a similar conclusion. Williams (1983: 391) places Hermann's insanity as early as Chapter III.

We have already noted how, at the Countess' funeral, Hermann 'crashed to the ground on his back' (247:9-10). If at the same time he hit his head on the stone floor, which admittedly is not stated but seems quite likely, he could well have incurred concussion or something worse. If we were to suppose that such a blow either precipitated or intensified his state of madness, as the case may be, it might then perfectly reasonably follow that the rest of the tale (that is to say the remainder of Chapter V, plus Chapter VI), taking in the ghostly visitation, the card games with Chekalinsky and the catastrophic outcome thereof, could be held to take place only within Hermann's fevered hallucinations. The only return to 'reality', if that be the case, would be the terse epilogue. This interpretation would allow the 'three-seven-ace' formula both to originate and to remain entirely within Hermann's consciousness until his babblings in the lunatic asylum. Such a reading does not, of course, square with the hoax theory tentatively outlined above: the two are at best incompatible alternatives (along with the fantastic reading and yet others).

The hoax theory allegedly breaks the rules by depending upon events outside the text (though, as we have seen, it is not alone among readings in doing this). What about the psychological reading just proposed? The only detail required from beyond the text would seem to be the hitting of the head – although it may be that even this is not absolutely necessary, if we posit an already deteriorating mental state for Hermann (from perhaps Chapter I onwards), exacerbated by imagining the corpse's diabolical wink. Perhaps Hermann only 'really' wakes up from that, or from the drunken stupor following his post-funeral dinner, in the asylum, his mind by then reduced to the continued utterance of gambling gabble. Williams (1983: 391) seems to come close to such a reading when he says 'but when Germann wakes up, *or thinks he wakes up*, after having left the funeral...' [my emphasis]. There is, of course, one further objection: the fact that Pushkin (or his narrator) fails to tell us this.

There may, however, be a precedent for such an omission from within the body of Pushkin's prose fiction. Pushkin's other purportedly supernatural tale is 'The Undertaker' ('*Grobovshchik*') from *The Tales of Belkin*. In this story the supposedly supernatural occurrence, involving a party for the undertaker's former clients (that is to say the dead), takes place in the protagonist's inebriated mind as he lies asleep. However, this fact is not apparent until near the end. The narration at the point of the story in question gives no clue of this: 'It was still dark outside when Adrian was aroused from his sleep', we are told; even later, the real explanation is given not by the narrator but by the undertaker's serving woman: 'Have you lost your mind or are you still befuddled by yesterday's wine?', she asks.[20] What we may have in *The Queen of Spades* therefore is a reversal of 'The Undertaker', in that the 'dream' (or delirium) is not announced as such at all. Narratorial non-inclusion as a device in Pushkin is not then confined to *The Queen of Spades*. However, just as commentators may have felt that this mode of composition does not exactly serve to enhance the artistic value of 'The Undertaker', so readers of *The Queen of Spades* may prefer not to deem this infinitely superior work to be dependent on such a crude ploy.

A variant to this type of psychological or realistic interpretation is the more psychoanalytical approach. We have seen that what might be called a vulgar Freudian reading, although possessing a few grains of substance, does not seem to have produced very satisfactory results. The Lacanian reading provided by Thomas (1992) is more interesting, but is still rather beset by the Oedipal complex and an obsession with primal scenes (here having to be transposed to the original card game of the 1760s). *The Queen of Spades* has been seen by some as essentially a psychological story, in the sense of it being a struggle for domination within the psyche of a single idea; it is also a struggle for the domination of Self (Hermann) over Other (or others: Countess, Lizaveta Ivanovna, the officer fraternity, society). It has frequently been observed that this is depicted in *The Queen of Spades* to a considerable extent in sexual terms and we have frequently noted the interplay within the work of sexual (or pseudo-sexual) imagery. Shvartsband (1988: 177) writes of Hermann's 'vision' (*videnie* – or the ghostly visitation) as a psychological mix of the heard, the desired and the fantasised, 'based on his guilt before the Countess and her ward'. We have also remarked on Rosen's interpretation of the imagery of Hermann's fantasising at the beginning of Chapter VI.

Debreczeny (1983: 232-8) provides a quite plausible near-psycho-analytical reading, with references to the Oedipal element, doors, passages (and rites thereof) and 'sexual' staircases (see again the reference to this in our hoax theory above). However, with the help of a few snippets from elsewhere, we may be able to add something to such an approach. Bocharov (1978: 316) has spoken of Hermann 'at the parting of the ways', having to make choices; Williams too (1989: 527) notes the 'alternatives offered in the tale'. The same critic has called Hermann a 'breaker of convention' (ibid.:

525); Falchikov (1977) terms him an 'outsider'. Part of Hermann's mission is to become an 'insider', a goal which he accomplishes both symbolically and literally when he manages to enter the Countess' house (Williams, 1983: 388).

Hermann's 'career' in *The Queen of Spades* can be seen as having an upward impetus, by various stages of what might be called 'games of two', up to the final climax. His trajectory is one of upward mobility, until his eventual catastrophic fall, Icarus-like, into a sea of madness. The twin impulses in his motivation would seem to be the attainment of wealth and sex: it is not entirely clear in which order, but both ultimately mean power and status (which arguably is anyway basically sexual, or indeed phallic, in nature). Hermann is thus engaged in an attempted penetration of society in an upward thrust to achieve satisfaction (status) at the highest level. This process is exposed throughout the text in a quite schematic, almost diagrammatic, manner.

The phrase 'game of two' combines the gaming motif central to the tale with the succession of dualities (in the form of choices and alternatives) with which Hermann's progress is faced. As we have seen already, in particular from fairy tale readings, he at key moments makes mistakes: that is to say, he makes the wrong choice, or takes the wrong turning, blinded by his obsessional ambition. Early on we are made aware of two poles within his psyche, vying for supremacy: one of caution and thrift and one of a gambling instinct. For a long time, it would seem, the former has dominated, while the latter pole has been accorded nothing beyond fascinated observation. Tomsky's anecdote of the three true cards, narrated while Hermann is engaged in this spectator sport, serves to tilt the balance. Hermann makes the unwise choice of pursuing an allegedly fabulous means of taking the gambling path in furtherance of his ultimate aspirations.

He contemplates sexual relations with the octogenarian Countess to facilitate acquisition of her secret; however, his discovery of the presence in the Countess' house of Lizaveta Ivanovna, an attractive young woman, presents him with two female alternatives through whom to negotiate his manoeuvres. He switches his attentions to Lizaveta Ivanovna and through her manages to gain clandestine admission to the house. Following Lizaveta's instructions, Hermann mounts the staircase and passes through a number of chambers until he is faced with two doors: the left one leads up to Lizaveta's room, the right one is the Countess' study. Hermann vacillates, then opts for the right door (Rowe, 1988: 149, points out that twice in the tale Hermann seems to choose the left option, but in fact goes for the right, with 'disastrous consequences'). Williams (1983: 388) has observed that 'to some extent the countess is "possessed" by [the usurper] Germann in this scene, as he enters her most intimate sanctuary and witnesses her most intimate moments'. Hermann, having made the wrong choice and destroyed the Countess (flashing his half-cocked pistol), belatedly takes the left door and the winding staircase, in some sense at very least then to possess Lizaveta. Following the trauma of the funeral, at which Hermann collapses and Lizaveta promptly faints, comes the ghostly visitation, supplying the purported secret of the cards and the injunction to marry Lizaveta. It is not clear in which order these instructions are to be carried out (or even that Hermann would *not* have married Lizaveta, had he achieved his financial goal); however the beginning of Chapter VI does insist that the card formula excluded all else from Hermann's mind. Here too his psyche must have made the wrong choice; he certainly somehow picks the wrong card in his third game with Chekalinsky (the ace lying to the left and the queen to the right). The disaster of this final 'game of two' precipitates mental collapse and so the usurping outsider, the interloper of German origin, receives his come-uppance.

Such a reading, of course, reduces (if that is the appropriate word) *The Queen of Spades* to the level of a psychological society tale, with psycho-analytical underpinnings: I omit here mention of the obvious Freudian details which are relatable to sexual taboo (mother fixation, wet nurses and so on).

Finally, let us tentatively put forward two proto-readings which may not yet have been fully elaborated, but which have been suggested in part by certain commentators, or for which some of the building blocks at least would seem to be in position. The first of these might be best placed within a category of 'social' readings; the second involves a more speculative or indeed poetic approach.

The first entails a combination of the method used by Lotman (1978) with certain of the ideas of Mikhail Bakhtin (the theoriser of polyphony in the novel, carnival and the chronotope). Bakhtin himself made only passing references to *The Queen of Spades*, in his celebrated study of Dostoevsky (first published in 1929). However he considered *The Queen of Spades* to be one the 'most carnivalised' of Pushkin's works and an important source for carnivalisation in *Crime and Punishment*.[21] In particular, Bakhtin singles out the Countess winking at Hermann from her coffin and sees the playing card, the queen of spades, as a sort of 'carnival double' of the old Countess (see Bakhtin, 1984: 159, 167). He also mentions Hermann's fainting in public at the Countess' funeral and notes the phenomenon of 'Napoleonism' within an 'early Russian capitalism' (ibid.: 168). *The Queen of Spades* as a tale seems to be, among other things, an utterance which has emerged from the social dialogue (to use Bakhtinian terms) of the 1820s and 30s, centering on attempted transgression or subversion of the social hierarchy. Gei (1989: 181) has commented of the tale that at times, with its exchanges of retorts, 'the narration moves in polyphonic bursts'. Pushkin has also established a strongly Bakhtinian chronotope (the literary intersection of time and space)

– the Petersburg winter night of the 1820s – which would be followed or emulated by Russian writers for at least the next hundred years.

A new article by Sally Dalton-Brown does use Bakhtin, but concentrates largely on generic questions, seeing *The Queen of Spades*, not unnaturally, as a mixture of genres and applying Bakhtin's favourite formula of the Menippean satire (many, at least, of the qualities of which, as outlined in Bakhtin, 1984, can be seen as applicable to Pushkin's tale). If *The Queen of Spades* is to be seen as a Menippean satire, then its relative brevity decrees that it must be regarded as a miniature model. Dalton-Brown (forthcoming) does go on to point up elements of carnival in the tale, suggesting that Hermann may be seen as a 'carnival king', the Countess as 'the ugly bride in a mock wedding (to death)' and Lizaveta as 'the jilted girl who becomes a carnival double of the Countess herself'; the whole is seen as 'both pattern and chaos, a gloriously parodic undermining of hubris by a jesting author'.

In his most recent book, *Universe of the Mind*, Lotman states that 'gambling embodies the outrageousness of outrageous life'; in connection with Dostoevsky's *The Gambler*, he draws a distinction between 'German caution and the Russian longing for instant ruin' (Lotman, 1990: 167). Hermann, the Russified German, could be seen as an early exemplar of this antithesis, or indeed a victim of its synthesis. He also posits a paradigmatic Pushkinian triangle comprising rebellious elements, a statue (or statuesque figure) and human being (ibid.: 85): in *The Queen of Spades* these roles are filled, on one level at least, by Hermann ('wild freedom'), the Countess (the relic, representing the status quo or 'dead captivity', who is 'turned to stone'), and Lizaveta (the duped but 'human' victim).

We have already seen from Lotman's seminal earlier article on card playing (Lotman, 1978) the semiotic significance of that activity as a modelling system for Russian society of the period. Card-playing, and especially a game of more or less pure chance such as faro, is itself a form of carnivalisation in which chaos can break out and fortunes rise or fall, mirroring or parallelling both 'games' of state, or high politics, and the social 'games' people play. Cards then are a form of carnivalised ritual which can result in hierarchical change: Hermann, had he been ultimately successful, would have been no mere shortlived carnival king; he would have transformed himself from German outsider to Russian *tuz* (ace).

Our final approach (as I would tentatively claim it to be, rather than a sustained or sustainable reading) in this study comes intrinsically from within romantic philosophy and its timeless antecedents in both thought and story, and from the more extrinsic trappings of contemporary Gothicism and freneticism. It has not been put forward as a coherent reading but, as usual, hints of such an approach are to be found among remarks made by a number of commentators. In addition, such a construction upon the story has been put, and creatively developed in his own works, by at least one leading present-day author.

We have seen already that Lotman (1978: 474) has discerned 'chains of characters' in successive works, linking Lizaveta, Hermann and the old Countess in *The Queen of Spades* with Sonia, Raskolnikov and the old money-lender in *Crime and Punishment*. Many Pushkin scholars, at least from the days of Slonimsky and Vinogradov, have drawn attention to the two historical periods which figure so prominently in the tale; Gukovsky, for instance (1957: 349), terms it 'a "montage" of scenes from two epochs'. Another of the more astute Soviet critics remarks that the compositional structure of the tale depends not on the juxtaposition of the two 'times', but lies in 'their conjunction in one temporal point' (Seleznev, 1974: 438). E.C. Barksdale (1979: 82, 151), consonant both with romantic philosophy and with his own brand of psychology, sees *The Queen of Spades* as a timeless myth in which space is 'simultaneously everywhere and nowhere'. Such ideas are only reinforced by the cyclical or repetitive nature of the story as brought out by the epilogic 'Conclusion'. Bayley (1971: 320) considers that 'the future is haunted by the past it has sought to exploit and profit by'.

In the light of such thoughts, we may now switch attention back to the characters, more in the fashion of Lotman's comment noted above. R.L. Busch (1987: 180), in his essay on 'Pushkin and the Gotho-freneticist tradition', refers to 'the archly freneticist device of contrasting the beautiful, vivacious countess of the 1770s, *la Vénus moscovite*, with the grotesquely moribund hag of the 1830s'. Another commentator, Joanna Hubbs (1988: 218), notes the opening of Chapter II, in which the Countess is seated in front of the looking glass, attended by three maids, 'like a goddess surrounded by attendants – or three "Fates" ', with Lizaveta Ivanovna, '*her youthful aspect*' [my emphasis], also waiting upon her from her embroidery frame. In fact the idea of this set-piece or tableau being reflected in the looking glass would serve to accentuate its framed pictorial quality, it being a well known feature of Renaissance painting that the presence of a young person alongside an elderly or moribund figure often denotes the 'youthful aspect' of that figure. In addition, of course, the next chapter presents us with an actual portrait, presumed to be that of the Countess in her youthful days, while we have already mentioned the likeness between this and the playing-card figure of the queen of spades, taken by Hermann for the Countess.

We now already have a possible confusion, or indeed alternatively a configuration, involving the old Countess, the young Countess and Lizaveta Ivanovna: a new triangle. As usual, Gareth Williams has some interesting and relevant observations. Commenting on the ambivalence of Hermann towards Lizaveta, he refers to her as 'a surrogate for that image of the young countess which fascinates his imagination', for whom also there is too, in his letters at least, 'a passion of the imagination' which comes and goes

(Williams, 1983: 387). Elsewhere, Williams states plainly that 'the countess, of course, is two persons', and again:

> The countess is a living alternative; she is both *la Vénus moscovite* of
> the 1770s and the old countess of the 1830s. This alternative becomes
> linked and even confused with the alternative between the fantastic
> and the real. (Williams, 1989: 528, 530)

Alternatives permeate the tale in this view: 'The dead countess may come alive. The countess may be both a beauty and a hag, Germann both a lover and a son...' (ibid.: 534, with an acknowledgement also to Barker, 1984: 202), as well as even a 'matricide' (Hubbs, 1988: 220).

Of course these alternatives cannot literally coexist within a realistic reading of the text. However, the possibilities for alternative mythic, psychological or hallucinatory interpretations must by now be long since apparent. If the Countess can, on some level, be two persons and she is closely linked to Lizaveta Ivanovna, a third, can all three conceivably be one? And this is where Carlos Fuentes enters the picture. Apart from his remarks on the character grouping of our trio – of Hermann, the Countess and Lizaveta Ivanovna (*vis-à-vis* Henry James and Dickens – Fuentes, 1988: 39) – he also develops the theme we have just been exploring, for which some of the ingredients at least do seem to be present within *The Queen of Spades*.

Among the cultural and personal factors that fed into the composition of story in his short novel *Aura* (1962), Fuentes lists Quevedo, Buñuel, a film by Mizoguchi, a story by the eighteenth-century Japanese writer Akinari and ultimately the ancient Chinese 'Biography of Ai'King'. Is there 'a book that is not the descendant of other books?' (ibid.: 38), the rhetorical question is posed. The common theme here is the ages of women, together with death and reunion; or, as Fuentes puts it (ibid.), 'that tide of narrative centuries that hardly begins to murmur the vastness of its constant themes: the supernatural virgin, the fatal woman, the spectral bride, the couple reunited'. One of the centuries to embrace such narratives with alacrity was of course that of the Gothic-Romantic age, at the tail end of which appeared *The Queen of Spades*; another is our own postmodern period of magical realism and neo-Gothicism. Carlos Fuentes, the Mexican novelist, is an outstanding exponent of this literary strain.[22]

In terms of character models or groupings, Fuentes names the Pushkin triangle, that of Henry James's *The Aspern Papers* and a certain trio from Dickens' *Great Expectations* (namely Miss Havisham, Estella and Pip). Without going into the merits of such a comparison here, let us say that it is the mysterious and tyrannical elderly women who interest Fuentes most, as being among 'the witches who consciously mothered Aura' (ibid.). Apart from the similar trios of characters (old woman, young woman and young man):

> In all three works the intruding young man wishes to know the old lady's secret: the secret of fortune in Pushkin, the secret of love in Dickens, the secret of poetry in James. The young girl is the deceiver – innocent or not – who must wrest the secret from the old woman before she takes it to the grave. (ibid.: 39)

Other female figures to feed into Fuentes' concept were Michelet's medieval sorceress (who preserved forbidden knowledge to the death), Circe (goddess of metamorphosis), the real life Maria Callas (whom Fuentes happened to meet days before her death, having seen and heard her sing in her glorious youth) and Marguerite Gautier (heroine of *La Dame aux camélias*, by Alexandre Dumas, *fils*, and of Verdi's *La Traviata*, which Callas had recorded). Again, the common factors are youth and age, death and beauty, sexuality and metamorphosis.

In his story *Aura*, Fuentes reverses the pattern he has detected in the three plots crudely sketched above ('a twist on machismo', he terms it: 39). Señora Consuelo, Aura and Felipe Montero become the trio in question; but 'Aura and Consuelo are *one*, and it is *they* who tear the scret of desire from Felipe's breast' (ibid.: Fuentes' emphasis). As in *The Queen of Spades* and the other works, the old woman and the young one are seen together in the same scenes, but in this version their actions when observed together tend to be the same: Aura is the one hundred and nine-year-old Consuela's much younger self or aura – about twenty in appearance – produced by occult means. Metamorphosis, amid an ambiance of shadows, mirrors and mirages, leads from ecstasy to horror.

In a literal sense, probably no one would suggest that Lizaveta Ivanovna and the old Countess are one person; but if, at some level at least, Lizaveta can be regarded as a surrogate for the young Countess, then the mythic and poetic relationship between Pushkin's tale and its descendant by Fuentes is clear. Somewhat similar connections can be seen between *The Queen of Spades* and other works, such as Daniil Kharms' long story 'The Old Woman' (1939), this time via *Crime and Punishment*. We have suggested earlier that retrospective readings (reading a work through later versions or adaptations of the same motifs) do not readily qualify as 'strong' readings. That may be so, but the re-working by Fuentes of the triangular and female situations suggested by Pushkin is so striking, as is the explicit revelation of his sources, that it does have the effect of sending the reader back to *The Queen of Spades* equipped with another dimension: one which, vestigially at least, does seem to be uncoverable in the original.

Given such a powerful recent creative impulse, sparked off at least in part by Pushkin's tale, and the ever-continuing interest in the work on the part of present-day scholarship, who can doubt that *The Queen of Spades* has life in her yet?

Notes to Part Two

1. For some reason, the Academy edition of Pushkin's works (Pushkin, 1948, see Bibliography) omits the epigraph to the work as a whole; see however other editions, such as that of Forsyth (1). A literal translation of the epigraph to Chapter I is as follows: 'And on nasty days/they gathered/ often:/they doubled [their stakes by "bending" their cards] – God forgive them! –/from fifty/to a hundred./And they would win away,/and mark it all down/ with chalk./Thus, on nasty days,/would they occupy themselves/with [serious] business. (Pushkin, 1948: 227).

2. Generally speaking it is here considered that, given the brevity of *The Queen of Spades* and the multiplicity of editions and translations, there is little need to cite page numbers; identification of words or passages can usually be readily made just from scenic description, or from chapter number. However, in this commentary section, exact reference is made, using the Pushkin 1948 edition, by page and line number in the text.

3. Hermann (in Russian 'Germann') is taken by Shvartsband (1988: 40) to be a surname; the usual asumption seems to be that it is a first name, with surname never given. We have already mentioned the doubling by Pushkin of the end 'n' and a possible explanation for that. In literary terms, it is often assumed to derive from Balzac's *L'Auberge rouge* of 1831 (Debreczeny, 1983: 208). The similarity of name with Saint-Germain has been noted (Shaw, 1962: 125 n.23; Kodjak, 1976: 103). Germann is of course a German; he and Saint-Germain 'are "germane", related psychologically if not biologically' (Schwartz and Schwartz, 1975: 281); and/or Saint-Germain is said to be 'both Hermann's *cousin*, and his spiritual, eighteenth-century and French father' (Doherty, 1992: 59).

4. *Mise en abyme*, a term taken from art history, and originally helraldry, refers to that corner, minute section, or sometimes mirror effect, of many a painting (or here that fragment of a literary work) in which the whole can be seen to have been encapsulated in miniature. The concept, if not the term itself, seems to have been first introduced into literary criticism by André Gide: see Ann Jefferson, *The Nouveau Roman and the Poetics of Fiction*, Cambridge University Press: Cambridge, 1980: 195-7; Linda Hutcheon, *Narcissitic Narrative: The Metafictional Paradox*, Methuen: London, 1984 (first published 1980) 9 and *passim*; Cornwell, 1990: 82.

5. 'Il paraiṭ que monsieur est décidément pour les suivantes./Que

voulez-vous, madame? Elles sont plus fraîches.' Davydov was astonished that Pushkin should have remembered these *bons mots* of his and exploited them, several years later, as an epigraph in *The Queen of Spades*.

6. Pike (unpublished) refers in support to a letter of Pushkin's of November 1824 on the great Petersburg flood of that year (depicted in *The Bronze Horseman*), in which he exclaims: 'Voilà une belle occasion à vos dames de Péterbourg de faire bidet'.

7. 'Princess Anna Fedotovna Tomski could have remarried after Prince Tomski's death and thus become Countess; in the first chapter Prince Paul Tomski calls his uncle "Count Ivan Ilich" and the fellow could conceivably be the Countess' son by the second marriage' (Nabokov and Barabtarlo, 1991: 60 n. 19).

8. Dante, *The Divine Comedy 3: Paradiso*, Canto XVII (ll. 61-9), Italian text with translation by John D. Sinclair, Oxford University Press: London, 1971: 244-5.

9. Pushkin appears to have been fond of such triadic aphorisms. In his piece 'On national drama and the play *Martha the Mayor's Wife*' he wrote: 'laughter, pity and horror are the three strings of our imagination' (quoted from Terts, 1975: 160).

10. It should perhaps be mentioned that the pun between 'Germann' and 'German' does not arise so readily in Russian, given that the Russian word for the national origin and language in question is *nemetskii* (and, like the noun *nemets*, a German, was originally connected with the modern word *nemoi*, meaning 'dumb').

11. Williams argues this more fully in an article (Williams: 1991-2) published too late (1993) for any proper consideration here. For more on the Voltaire epigraph, see Williams, 1989: 533-4.

12. The petrification of the old woman (*okamenev*, 245: 29) has led to links being made with the theme of the statuesque in Pushkin (see Lotman, 1990: 85; Shapiro, 1979: 124, who sees 'the playing card-come-to-life' as analogous). The statue in Pushkin is examined (without reference to *The Queen of Spades*) by Roman Jakobson, 'The Statue in Puškin's Poetic Mythology', in his *Language in Literature*, edited by Krystyna Pomorska and Stephen Rudy (Belknap Press: Cambridge, MA, 1987) 318-67 and 525-9 (earlier published in Czech in 1937; and as *Puškin and His Sculptural Myth*, Mouton: The Hague, 1975).

13. The phrase 'young bishop' (*molodoi arkhierei*) is a late alteration to the text; the original publication used the phrase 'excellent preacher' (*slavnyi propovednik*): see Pushkin, 1940: 837.

14. ' –*Attendez!* / – How dare you say *attendez* to me? / – Your excellency, I said *attendez* sir!' (249).

15. The Russian word *dama*, apart from meaning 'lady' or (in cards) 'queen', can also mean a (dance) partner; Barker (1984: 207) suggests it can

signify 'wife', thus strengthening indications of Hermann's sexual interest in the Countess.

16. On *The Queen of Spades* as a source for Henry James's story *The Aspern Papers*, see: Briggs, 1972; Fuentes, 1988; and, for a full discussion, Cornwell, 1990: 113-39. An argument could also be made for *The Queen of Spades* as a source for another James story, *The Figure in the Carpet*. The case cannot be made in detail here, but both stories feature a manic quest to discover a secret that may or may not exist; the quest becomes an obsession, sliding into madness. In Pushkin, the secret is disclosed, but it may or may not have authenticity. In James it is not disclosed, at least not to the narrator; the people to whom it is allegedly disclosed refuse to disclose it to him; the authenticity of its disclosure, and indeed of its very existence, remain in doubt. James has transformed the gambling secret and milieu to a critical 'point' and a literary circle; the Hermann figure has become James' narrator and the writer, Vereker, has assumed the role of the Countess. Other, more minor, characters can be seen in parallel. *The Figure in the Carpet* is further, in terms of configuration of characters and plot functions, from *The Queen of Spades* than is *The Aspern Papers*, but the basic idea is similar – indeed perhaps even closer; the development of the plot depends on a series of 'misreadings' of a basic anecdote; a number of textual details in James (as with *Aspern*) are reminiscent of, and indeed may allude to, Pushkin; and sexual inadequacy is somehow at the heart of all three tales.

17. 'Architext' (or *architextualité*) is Genette's term to denote a broader (generic) range of intertextual reference (as opposed to a single intertextual source): see Gérard Genette, *Introduction à l' architexte* (Seuil: Paris, 1979).

18. See note 19 to Part One (Introduction). See also Petrunina, 1980; Reeder, 1982; and Cornwell, 1990 (for the tracing of parallel plot functions in James' *The Aspern Papers*: see also note 16 above).

19. See on this Todorov (cited above in note 3 to Part One, Introduction); and the theoretical section of Cornwell, 1990.

20. Quoted from *Alexander Pushkin: Complete Prose Fiction*, translated by Paul Debreczeny (Stanford University Press: Stanford, 1983) 90, 92.

21. Carnivalisation in literature is seen as occurring in literary texts or scenes (including dreams) which subvert the status quo or standard values, involving role reversal, popular humour and incongruous, but potentially liberating, mixes (e.g. of the sacred and profane). See Chapter 4 of Bakhtin, 1984; plus Bakhtin's *Rabelais and His World*, translated by Hélène Iswolsky (MIT Press: Cambridge, MA, 1968; reprinted Indiana University Press: Bloomington, 1984; original published 1965).

22. Apart from *Aura*, Fuentes makes use of the same motif again in his masterpiece, the novel *Terra Nostra* (1975; English translation 1976). An apparent imitation, probably deriving from Fuentes, is to be found in the 'Argentina' scene of Salman Rushdie's *The Satanic Verses* (1988).

Bibliography

Primary sources

Aleksandr Pushkin, *Polnoe sobranie sochinenii* (Academy of Sciences: Moscow-Leningrad, 1937-59: vol. 8, 1948) 227-52.
Variants are to be found in vol. 8: 2, 1940: 834-7.
A.S. Pushkin, *Pikovaia Dama/The Queen of Spades*, James Forsyth (ed.) (Bristol Classical Press: Bristol, 1992; formerly Bradda Books: Letchworth, 1963; Blackwell's Russian Texts: Oxford, 1984).

Some English translations

Alexander Pushkin, *The Queen of Spades and Other Stories*, translated by Rosemary Edmonds (Penguin Books: Harmondsworth, 1962) 151-83. Also in: Alberto Manguel, *Black Water: The Anthology of Fantastic Literature* (Picador: London, 1983) 478-502.
The Complete Prose Tales of Alexandr Sergeyevitch Pushkin, translated by Gillon R. Aitken (Michael Russell: Salisbury, 1978) 273-305; (first published by Barrie and Rockliff, 1966; republished by Vintage: London, 1993).
Alexander Pushkin, *Complete Prose Fiction*, translated by Paul Debreczeny (Stanford University Press: Stanford, 1983) 211-33.
Russian 19th-century Gothic Tales (Raduga Publishers: Moscow, 1984), translated by Ivy and Tatiana Litvinov, 179-206.
The Ardis Anthology of Russian Romanticism, Christine Rydel (ed.) (Ardis: Ann Arbor, 1984), translated by Carl R. Proffer, 311-25.

Secondary sources

(see also the bibliographies to Debreczeny, 1983: 260-4, below; and Proffer and Meyer, 1990)

Akhmatova, Anna, *Sochineniia v dvukh tomakh*, vol. 2 (1986) (Khudozhestvennaia literatura: Moscow; notes to 1958-9 supplement to ' "Kamennyi gost' " Pushkina' of 1958).

Alekseev, M.P., 'Pushkin i nauka ego vremeni', in his *Pushkin: sravnitel' no-istoricheskie issledovaniia* (Nauka: Leningrad, 1984) 22-173, 110-25. First published 1956.

Bakhtin, Mikhail, *Problems of Dostoevsky's Poetics*, translated by Caryl Emerson (ed.) (Manchester University Press: Manchester, 1984). First Russian edition 1929, enlarged 1963.

Barker, Adele, 'Pushkin's *Queen of Spades*: A Displaced Mother Figure', *American Imago* 41, 2 (1984) 201-9.

Barksdale, E.C., *Daggers of the Mind: Structuralism and neuropsychology in an exploration of the Russian literary imagination* (Coronado Press: Lawrence, Kansas, 1979) 76-83.

Bayley, John, *Pushkin: A comparative commentary* (Cambridge University Press: Cambridge, 1971) 316-24.

Belinskii, V. G., *Polnoe sobranie sochinenii*, vol. VII (Gos. izd. Khodozhest-vennoi literatury: Moscow, 1955) 577.

Berkovskii, N. Ia. (1987). See M.N. Virolainen (below).

Bobrova, E.I., 'Perevod P. Merime "Pikovoi damy" (Avtograficheskaia rukopis')', in *Pushkin: issledovaniia i materialy* 2 (1958) 354-61.

Bocharov, S.G., 'The Queen of Spades', *New Literary History*, vol. 9 (1978) 315-32, translated by Ann Feltham; from Bocharov's *Poetika Pushkina: ocherki* (Nauka: Moscow, 1974) 186-206.

Botnikova, A.B., *E.T.A. Gofman i russkaia literatura* (Izdatel'stvo Voronezh-skogo universiteta: Voronezh, 1977) 98-106.

Briggs, A.D.P., 'Alexander Pushkin: a possible influence on Henry James', *Forum for Modern Language Studies* vol. VIII, 1 (1972) 52-61.

———— '*Pikovaya dama* and *Taman*: Questions of kinship', *Journal of Russian Studies* 37 (1979) 13-20.

———— *Alexander Pushkin: A critical study* (Croom Helm: London, 1983: 218-24; reprinted by Bristol Classical Press, Bristol, 1991).

Brown, William Edward, *A History of Russian Literature of the Romantic Period* vol. 3 (Ardis: Ann Arbor, 1986) 218-24.

Budgen, David, 'Pushkin and the Novel', in *From Pushkin to 'Palisandriia': Essays on the Russian Novel in Honour of Richard Freeborn*, Arnold McMillin (ed.) (Macmillan: Basingstoke and London, 1990) 3-38.

Burgin, Diana Lewis, 'The mystery of "Pikovaja Dama": A new interpreta-tion', in *Mnemozina: Studia litteraria russica in honorem Vsevolod Setchkarev*, Joachim T. Baer and Norman W. Ingham (eds) (Fink: Munich, 1974) 46-56.

Busch, R.L., 'Pushkin and the Gotho-freneticist Tradition', *Canadian Slavonic Papers* June-September (1987) 165-83.

Chkhaidze, L.V., 'O real'nom znachenii motiva trekh kart v "Pikovoi dame"', in *Pushkin; issledovaniia i materialy* 3 (1960) 455-60.

Chukovskaia, Lidiia, *Zapiski ob Anne Akhmatove*, vol. 1 (YMCA Press:

Paris, 1976).

Clayton, J. Douglas, *'Spadar Dame, Pique-Dame*, and *Pikovaia dama*: A German Source for Pushkin?', *Germano-Slavica* 4 (1974) 5-10.

Cornwell, Neil, *The Literary Fantastic: from Gothic to Postmodernism* (Harvester Wheatsheaf: New York and London, 1990) 113-39.

Dalton-Brown, Sally, 'Menippean Violations, Carnival Chaos: Defining the genre of Pushkin's "Pikovaia dama" ', *Russian Literature* (forthcoming).

Davydov, Sergei, 'Real'noe i fantasticheskoe v *Pikovoi dame*', *Revue des études slaves* 59, 1-2 (1987) 263-7.

Debreczeny, Paul, 'Poetry and Prose in "The Queen of Spades" ', *Canadian–American Slavic Studies* 11 (1977) 91-113.

———— *The Other Pushkin: A study of Alexander Pushkin's Prose Fiction* (Stanford University Press: Stanford, 1983) 186-238.

Doherty, Justin, 'Fictional Paradigms in Pushkin's "Pikovaya dama" ', *Essays in Poetics* 17:1 (1992) 49-66.

Dostoevskii, F.M., *Polnoe sobranie sochinenii*, vol. 30, kn. 1-aia (Nauka: Leningrad, 1988) 192.

Emerson, Caryl,' "The Queen of Spades" and the Open End', in *Puškin Today*, David Bethea (ed.) (Indiana University Press: Bloomington, 1992) 20-6.

Esipov, V., 'Istoricheskii podtekst v povesti Pushkina "Pikovaia dama" ', *Voprosy literatury* 4 (1989) 193-205.

Falchikov, M., 'The Outsider and the Number Game (Some observations on *Pikovaya dama)*', *Essays in Poetics* 2:2 (1977) 96-106.

Faletti, Heidi E., 'Remarks on Style as Manifestation of Narrative Technique in "The Queen of Spades" ', *Canadian–American Slavic Studies* 11, no. 1 (Spring, 1977) 114-33.

Forsyth, James, Introduction to A.S. Pushkin, *Pikovaya dama/The Queen of Spades* (Bradda: Letchworth, 1963: reprinted Blackwell, 1985; Bristol Classical Press, 1992) vii-xxv.

Fuentes, Carlos, 'How I Wrote One of My Books', in his *Myself With Others: Selected Essays* (André Deutsch: London, 1988) 28-45. Reprinted as 'How I Wrote Aura', in Carlos Fuentes, *Aura*, translated by Lysander Kemp (André Deutsch: London, 1990).

Gei, N.K., *Proza Pushkina: poetika povestvovaniia* Chapter IV: 'Pikovaia dama' (Nauka: Moscow, 1989) 173-95.

Gershenzon, M., *Mudrost' Pushkina* (Ardis: Ann Arbor, 1983; reprint of Moscow, 1919 edition) 97-112.

Gourg, Marianne, '*La Dame de pique* dans les miroirs de Gogol' ', *Revue des études slaves* 59, 1-2 (1987) 269-76.

Gregg, Richard A., 'Balzac and the Women in *The Queen of Spades*', *Slavic and East European Journal* X, 3 (1966) 279-82.

Gronicka, André von, *The Russian Image of Goethe. Volume I: Goethe in*

82 Pushkin's *The Queen of Spades*

8888

Russian Literature of the First Half of the Nineteenth Century (University of Philadelphia Press: Philadelphia, 1968) 66-7.

Gukovskii, G.A., *Pushkin i problemy realisticheskogo stilia* (Gos. izd. khodozhestvennaia literatura, 1957) 340-67.

Henry, Hélène, 'Note sur les traductions en français de *La Dame de pique*', *Revue des études slaves* 59, 1-2 (1987) 277-84.

Hubbs, Joanna, *Mother Russia: The feminine myth in Russian culture* (Indiana University Press: Bloomington and Indianapolis, 1988) 207-27.

Iakubovich, D., 'O "Pikovoi dame", in his *Pushkin: 1833 god* (Pushkinskoe obshchestvo: Leningrad, 1933) 57-68.

———— 'Literaturnyi fon "Pikovoi damy" (Diukanzh, Fan-der-Vel'de)', *Literaturnyi sovremennik* 1 (1935) 206-12.

———— 'Literaturnyi fon "Pikovoi damy" ', with an introduction by Alexander Gribanov, *The Pushkin Journal* (forthcoming).

Ingham, Norman W., *E.T.A. Hoffmann's Reception in Russia* (jal-verlag: Würzburg, 1974) 134-40.

Katz, Michael R., 'Dreams in Pushkin', *California Slavic Studies* XI (1980) 71-103.

Khodasevich, V., 'Peterburgskie povesti Pushkina', in his *Stat'i o russkoi poezii* (Prideaux Press: Letchworth, 1971: 58-96; first published 1922; dated 1914).

Kodjak, Andrej, ' "The Queen of Spades" in the context of the Faust legend', in *Alexander Puškin: A symposium of the 175th anniversary of his birth*, Andrej Kodjak and Kiril Taranovsky (eds) (New York University Press: New York, 1976) 87-118.

Kupreanova, E.N. (ed.), *Istoriia russkoi literatury. Vol. II. Ot sentimentalizma k romantizmu i realizmu* (Nauka: Leningrad, 1981).

Labriolle, F. de, 'Le "Secret des trois cartes" dans la "Dame de Pique" de Pushkin', *Canadian Slavonic Papers* 11, 2 (1969) 261-71.

Leatherbarrow, W.J., 'Pushkin: The Queen of Spades', in *The Voice of A Giant: Essays on seven Russian prose classics*, Roger Cockrell and David Richards (eds) (University of Exeter: Exeter, 1985) 1-14.

Leighton, Lauren G., 'Numbers and numerology in "The Queen of Spades"', *Canadian Slavonic Papers* 19 (1977A) 417-43.

———— 'Gematria in "The Queen of Spades": A Decembrist puzzle', *Slavic and East European Journal* 21, 4 (1977B) 455-69.

———— 'Puškin and Freemasonry: "The Queen of Spades" ', in *New Perspectives on Nineteenth-Century Russian Prose*, George J. Gutsche and Lauren G. Leighton (eds) (Slavica: Columbus, Ohio, 1982) 15-25.

Lerner, N.O., 'Istoriia "Pikovoi damy"', in his *Rasskazy o Pushkine* (Priboi: Leningrad, 1929) 132-63.

Lezhnëv, A., *Pushkin's Prose*, translated by Roberta Reeder (Ardis: Ann Arbor, 1983: *passim*.; original published 1937).

Lotman, Jurij M., 'Theme and Plot: The theme of cards and the card game in Russian literature of the nineteenth century', translated by C.R. Pike, *PTL* 3 (1978) 455-92; first published 1975.

—————— *Universe of the Mind: A Semiotic Theory of Culture*, translated by Ann Shukman (I.B. Tauris & Co.: London, 1990).

Makogonenko, G.P., *Tvorchestvo A.S. Pushkina v 1830-e gody (1833-1836)* (Khodozhestvennaia literatura: Moscow, 1982).

Mann, Iu., *Poetika Gogolia* (Khudozhestvennaia literatura: Moscow, 1978) 67-70.

Mersereau, John, Jr, *Russian Romantic Fiction* (Ardis: Ann Arbor, 1983) 221-6.

—————— In *The Cambridge History of Russian Literature*, Charles A. Moser (ed.) (Cambridge University Press: Cambridge, 1989) 175-7.

Mil'china, V.A., 'Zapiski "Pikovoi damy" ', *Vremennik Pushkinskoi komissii*, vypusk 22 (Leningrad: Nauka, 1988) 136-42.

Mirsky, D.S., *A History of Russian Literature*, abridged by Francis J. Whitfield (ed.) (Alfred A. Knopf: New York, 1958; first published 1926).

Mirsky, Prince D.S., *Pushkin* (Haskell House: New York, 1974: 183-6; first published 1926).

Moser, Charles A. (ed.), *The Cambridge History of Russian Literature* (Cambridge University Press: Cambridge, 1989).

Murav'eva, O.S., ' "Pikovaia dama" v issledovaniiakh poslednego desiatiletiia', *Russkaia literatura* 3 (1977) 219-28.

—————— 'Fantastika v povesti Pushkina "Pikovaia dama" ', in *Pushkin: issledovaniia i materialy* vol. 8 (1978) 62-9.

Nabokov, Vera, and Barabtarlo, Gennady, 'A possible source for Pushkin's "Queen of Spades" ' *RLT* 24 (1991) 43-62.

Nabokov, Vladimir, Commentary to Aleksandr Pushkin, *Eugene Onegin: A novel in verse*, translated by Vladimir Nabokov, 4 vols, *passim.* (Routledge: London; Princeton University Press: Princeton, 1964).

Passage, Charles E., *The Russian Hoffmannists* (Mouton & Co.: The Hague, 1963) 131-9.

Petrunina, N.N., 'Pushkin i traditsiia volshebnoskazachnogo povestvovaniia (k poetike "Pikovoi damy")', *Russkaia literatura* 3 (1980) 30-50.

—————— 'Dve "Petersburgskie povesti" Pushkina', in *Pushkin: issledovaniia i materialy*, vol. X (Nauka: Leningrad, 1982) 147-67.

—————— 'Proza Pushkina i puti ego evoliutsii', *Russkaia literatura* 1 (1987A) 40-60.

—————— 'Poetika filosofskoi povesti', in her *Proza Pushkina (puti evoliutsii)* (Nauka: Leningrad, 1987B) 199-240.

Phillips, Delbert D., *Spook or Spoof? The structure of the supernatural in Russian Romantic tales* (University Press of America: Washington, DC, 1982) 99-106.

Pike, C.R., 'Alexander Pushkin's "The Queen of Spades" and the beginnings of Russian prose fiction'. Unpublished paper.

Poliakova, E., ''Real'nost' i fantastika "Pikovoi damy" ', in *V mire Pushkina: sbornik statei* (Sovetskii pisatel': Moscow, 1974) 373-412.

Proffer, Carl R., and Meyer, Ronald, *Nineteenth-Century Russian Literature in English: A bibliography of criticism and translations* (Ann Arbor: Ardis, 1990) 122-38.

Pursglove, Michael, 'Chronology in Pushkin's *Pikovaya dama*', *Irish Slavonic Studies* 6 (1985) 11-18.

Raskolnikoff, Felix, 'Irratsional'noe v *Pikovoi dame*', *Revue des études slaves* 59, 1-2 (1987) 247-61.

Reeder, Roberta, 'The Queen of Spades: A parody of the Hoffmannian tale', in *New Perspectives on Nineteenth-Century Rusian Prose*, George J. Gutsche and Lauren G. Leighton (eds) (Slavica: Columbus, Ohio, 1982) 73-98.

Reid, Robert (ed.), *Problems of Russian Romanticism* (Gower: Aldershot, 1986).

Remizov, Aleksei, *Ogon' veshchei* (Sovetskaia Rossiia: Moscow, 1989: 148-9). First published 1954.

Roberts, Carolyn, 'Puškin's "Pikovaja dama" and the Opera Libretto', *Canadian Review of Comparative Literature* 6 (1979) 9-26.

Rosen, Nathan, 'The Magic Cards in The Queen of Spades', *Slavic and East European Journal* 19, 3 (1975) 255-75.

———— 'The Magic Cards: A Correction', *Slavic and East European Journal* 21 (1977) 301-2.

Rowe, W.W., *Patterns in Russian Literature II: Notes on classics* (Ardis: Ann Arbor, 1988) 147-54.

Ryan, W.F., and Wigzell, Faith, 'Gullible Girls and Dreadful Dreams. Zhukovskii, Pushkin and Popular Divination', *The Slavonic and East European Review* 70, 4 (1992) 647-69.

Schwartz, Murray M., and Schwartz, Albert, ' "The Queen of Spades": A psychoanalytic interpretation', *Texas Studies in Literature and Language* XVII (1975) 275-88.

Seleznev, Iu., 'Proza Pushkina i razvitie russkoi literatury (k poetike siuzheta)', in *V mire Pushkina: sbornik statei* (Sovetskii pisatel': Moscow, 1974) 413-46.

Shapiro, Michael, 'Pushkin's Modus Signifikandi: A Semiotic Exploration', in *Russian Romanticism: Studies in the Poetic Codes*, Nils Ake Nilsson (ed.) (Almqvist & Wiksell: Stockholm, 1979) 110-34.

Sharypkin, D.M., 'Vokrug "Pikovoi damy" ', *Vremennik Pushkinskoi komissii*, 1972 (published 1974) 128-38.

Shaw, Joseph T., 'The "Conclusion" of Pushkin's *Queen of Spades*' in *Studies in Russian and Polish Literature: In honor of Waclaw Lednicki*

Zbigniew Folejewski *et al.* (eds) (Mouton: The Hague, 1962) 114-26.

Shklovskii, Viktor, 'Pikovaia dama' in his *Zametki o proze Pushkina* (Sovetskii pisatel': Moscow, 1937) 53-74.

Shklovsky, V., 'Notes on Pushkin's Prose. A Society Tale: *The Queen of Spades*', in *Russian Views of Pushkin*, translated by D.J. Richards and C.R.S. Cockrell (eds) (Willem A. Meeuws: Oxford, 1976: 187-95; excerpted from Shklovskii, 1937).

Shrayer, Maxim D., 'Rethinking Romantic Irony: Puškin, Byron, Schlegel and *The Queen of Spades*', *Slavic and East European Journal* 36, 4 (1992) 397-414.

Shukman, Ann, 'The short story: Theory, analysis, interpretation', *Essays in Poetics* 2:2 (1977) 27-95.

Shvartsband, S., *Logika khudozhestvennogo poiska A.S. Pushkina ot "Ezerskogo" do "Pikovoi damy"* (The Magnes Press: Jerusalem, 1988).

Sidiakov, L.S., 'Pushkin i razvitie russkoi povesti v nachale 30-kh godov XIX veka', in *Pushkin: issledovaniia i materialy* 3 (1960) 193-217.

Simpson, Mark S., 'Aleksandr Pushkin's *The Queen of Spades*', in his *The Russian Gothic Novel and its British Antecedents* (Slavica: Columbus, Ohio, 1986) 51-63.

Slonimskii, A., *Masterstvo Pushkina*, 2nd edn (Gos. izd. Khodozhestvennoi literatury: Moscow, 1963) 519-25.

Terras, Victor, *A History of Russian Literature* (Yale University Press: New Haven and London, 1991).

Terts, Abram [Andrei Siniavskii], *Progulki s Pushkinym* (Overseas Publications Interchange, in association with Collins: London, 1975).

Thomas, Alfred, 'A Russian Oedipus: Lacan and Puškin's "The Queen of Spades" ', *Wiener Slawistischer Almanach* 31 (1992) 47-59.

Tomashevskii, B.V., 'Ritm prozy ("Pikovaia dama")', in his *O stikhe: stat' i* (Priboi: Leningrad, 1929) 254-318.

Vilenchik, B. Ia., 'Istoricheskoe proshloe v "Pikovoi dame" ', *Vremennik Pushkinskoi komissii 1981* (Leningrad: Nauka, 1985) 173-9.

Vinogradov, V.V., 'Stil' "Pikovoi damy" ' and '[O "Pikovoi dame"] Iz knigi "Stil' Pushkina" ', in his *O iazyke khudozhestvennoi prozy: izbrannye trudy* (Nauka: Moscow, 1980: 176-239; 256-83). First published 1936; 1941.

Virolainen, M.N., 'N.Ia. Berkovskii. O "Pikovoi dame" (Zametki iz arkhiva)', *Russkaia literatura* 1 (1987) 61-9.

Weber, Harry B., '*Pikovaja dama*: A case for Freemasonry in Russian literature', *Slavic and East European Journal* XII, 4 (1968) 435-47.

Williams, Gareth, 'Pushkin and Jules Janin: A contribution to the literary background of "The Queen of Spades" ', *Quinquereme* IV:2 (1981) 206-24.

——— 'The Obsessions and Madness of Germann in *Pikovaja dama*',

Russian Literature XIV (1983) 383-96.

——— 'Convention and play in *Pikovaja dama*', *Russian Literature* XXVI (1989) 523-38.

——— 'Otgoloski otnosheniia Punshkina k Aleksandru I v epigrafakh k "Pikovoi dame" ', *Studia Slavica Hungarica* 37 (1991-2) 287-95 (published 1993).

Wolff, Tatiana, *Pushkin on Literature* (Methuen: London, 1971).

Žekulin, Gleb, 'And in Conclusion, Who is Tomsky? (Rereading "The Queen of Spades")', *Zapiski russkoi akademicheskoi gruppy v S ShA* vol. XX (1987) 71-9.

Addendum to the Second Edition

Gregg, Richard, 'Germann the Confessor and the Stony, Seated Countess: The Moral Subtext of *The Queen of Spades*', *Slavonic and East European Review*, 78, 4 (2000), 612-24.

Grenier, Svetlana, ' "Everyone Knew Her..." or Did They? Rereading Pushkin's Lizaveta Ivanovna ("The Queen of Spades")', *Canadian Slavonic Papers*, 38, 1-2 (1996), 93-107.

Krasukhin, Genadii, *Pushkin. Boldino. 1833* (Izdatel'stvo "FLINTA": Moscow, 1997).

Leighton, Lauren G., *The Esoteric Tradition in Russian Romantic Literature: Decembrism and Freemasonry* (The Pennsylvania State University Press: University Park, Pennsylvania, 1994).

Rosenshield, Gary, 'Choosing the Right Card: Madness, Gambling, and the Imagination in Pushkin's "The Queen of Spades"', *PMLA* 109 (1994), 995-1008.

——— 'Freud, Lacan, and Romantic Psychoanalysis: Three Psychoanalytic Approaches to Madness in Pushkin's *The Queen of Spades*', *Slavic and East European Journal*, 40, 1 (1996), 1-26.

Shmid, Volf [Wolf Schmid], ' "Pikovaia dama" kak metatekstual'naia novella', in his *Proza kak poeziia*, second edition: (INAPRESS: St Petersburg, 1998) 103-44; shorter version in *Russkaia literatura* 3 (1997) 6-28.

Whitehead, Claire, 'The Fantastic in Russian Romantic Prose: Pushkin's *The Queen of Spades*', in *The Gothic-Fantastic in Nineteenth-Century Russian Literature*, Neil Cornwell (ed.) (Rodopi: Amsterdam and Atlanta, Georgia, 1999), 103-25.

Translation

Alexander Pushkin, *The Queen of Spades and Other Stories*, translated by Alan Myers, edited by Andrew Kahn (Oxford University Press: Oxford, 1997), 69-100.

Appendix

A note on the Count Saint-Germain

> You have heard of the Count Saint-Germain, of whom so much that is wonderful is said. You know that he gave himself out to be the Wandering Jew, the discoverer of the elixir of life and the philosopher's stone, and so on. He was ridiculed as a charlatan and Casanova says in his memoirs that he was a spy....
>
> *(The Queen of Spades*, 228:32-7)

Of the various historical personages appearing in or alluded to in Pushkin's *The Queen of Spades*, indisputedly the most important, and the most intriguing, is the Count Saint-Germain (or *M. le comte de Saint-Germain*). Saint-Germain was still known, and even still remembered, in European aristocratic circles in Pushkin's time and Pushkin clearly knew of him both by hearsay and through Casanova's memoirs, apart from other possible sources. He appears also in a work by V.F. Odoevsky (first published in 1839). He was the subject of an English historical novel by George R. Preedy, published in 1942. Recently he has made a fictional reappearance in Umberto Eco's novel *Foucault's Pendulum*. The nearest thing to a biography would seem to be a book by Isabel Cooper-Oakley, first published in Italy in 1912, and written very much from the theosophical persuasion (with a foreword by Annie Besant, quoting liberally from Madame Blavatsky and dedicated to 'The Great Soul who in the struggles of the eighteenth century worked, suffered and triumphed').

As Pushkin wrote, 'Saint-Germain, despite his mysteriousness, was of very respectable appearance and in society was a very charming man' (228:37-9). So much so that, according to another source, he 'passed through the drawing rooms of all Europe' (Givry: 365). In so doing, he provoked various reactions. Certain members of high society evidently held him in a kind of religious awe; he seemed to have a particularly striking effect on women, from Madame de Pompadour to Catherine the Great's mother, though there seems little evidence that he exploited this sexually. He made enemies of some, but by no means all, political figures (he seems to have been a great friend of Grigorii Orlov, Catherine's favourite). In others he provoked ridicule: a certain Count Warnstedt described him in 1779, towards the end of his 'career', as 'the completest charlatan, fool, rattle-pate, wind-bag and swindler' (Wilson: 411).

His life is still virtually a complete mystery from beginning to end. He seems to have had no known first names (Eco's imposition of the name Claude-Louis may be either fictitious or erroneous), though he did go under many a (titled) alias (such as Count Weldon, sometimes spelt 'Welldone' or 'Welldown' and Count Soltikoff, among others). He should not be, but often is, confused with the real French family of Saint-Germain (notably with his close contemporary Count Robert de Saint-Germain, 1708-78, French sol-dier and Minister of War). According to Oakley, at least, even further confusion and yet more apocrypha were occasioned by the predilection of a certain Englishman, one Lord Gower, for impersonating our Saint-Germain over the length and breadth of Europe. What little sense that can be made of his life and career is scarcely beyond the class of Tomsky's anecdote.

There are various versions of his birth. The one favoured by his strong supporters is that he was descended from Franz-Leopold, Prince Ragoczy of Transylvania (he sometimes went as 'Graf Tzarogy' or 'Ragotsy'), who died in 1734, having opposed the Austrian Empire. He may have been the third son (born perhaps in 1710 or perhaps even in the 1690s, not to mention rumours of his having attended the marriage at Cana, while one of Eco's epigraphs suggests that he knew Pontius Pilate!). On hearing that his elder brothers had taken saints' names, he called himself 'Sanctus Germano, the Holy Brother' (Oakley: 11). Alternatively, he may have been 'the son of a tax collector of San Germano' in Savoy (Wilson: 409), a 'Portuguese Jew', or virtually anything. He spoke a number of languages fluently, or even perfectly, including according to some accounts oriental tongues, and French 'with a Piedmontese accent'. He may have studied at the University of Siena, under the protection of the Medici family, and/or he may have travelled widely in the East. First reliable sightings of him seem to date from the 1740s, though some old ladies claimed to have met him in Venice as early as 1710, when allegedly even then he appeared, as he constantly did for the rest of the century, to be aged between forty and fifty. His heyday would seem to have been in Paris, under Louis XV and Madame de Pompadour, in the late 1750s. A failed and dubious diplomatic mission to The Hague in 1760, to which Casanova's comment refers, seems to have marked a downward turning point in his career.

In Russia in 1762 Saint-Germain was befriended by the Orlov family. He had been close to Catherine's mother in Paris; seemingly he involved himself in Russian political events, lived in St Petersburg with 'Count Rotari, the famous Italian painter' and 'was staying with Princess Marie Galitzin at Archangelskoi on March 3rd, 1762' (Oakley: 19-20 and 41-2). This must surely have been a relation of the future husband of Pushkin's prototype for the Countess (from 1766 Princess Natal'ia Petrovna Golitsyna), although there may be no clear evidence as to whether Pushkin was aware of this detail.

Saint-Germain was certainly a highly-educated, sophisticated and gifted conversationalist who spread bizarre rumours of both his antiquity and his powers. He was an accomplished musician, apparently of unlimited but mysterious wealth, an occult scholar, a fanatical chemist, an alchemical adept and a brilliant dyer and mixer of colours (to a secret formula which he refused to divulge). Another of his interests of possible Pushkinian relevance was the Pythagorean School and 'Numbers' (Oakley: 147). He seems to have been a prominent Freemason (though this has been denied: see Wilson: 413), Rosicrucian and Knight Templar. He continued to receive patronage in various courts and castles of Europe and made occasional reappearances in Paris (1761, 1770 and the 1780s), allegedly bringing dire but unheeded warnings of the Revolution to come. Cagliostro became his pupil, which fact may have led to a version of Saint-Germain's own demise in the dungeons of the Inquisition (Givry: 365).

The standard version of Saint-Germain's death is that he expired at a castle at Eckenförde in Holstein in 1784. However, this does not appear to have prevented his attendance at a top Masonic gathering in Paris in 1785! Further sightings of him are reported both before and during the French Revolution and even in subsequent centuries. Theories as to his longevity are also divided: between the Wandering Jew, or Melmoth the Wanderer, variety and reincarnation.

One last point of interest, which would bring a glow to the cheeks of Andrej Kodjak. Oakley (54, 90 and 92-3) quotes extensively from the *Souvenirs sur Marie-Antoinette* by the Countess d'Adhémar (Paris, 1836). This person claimed to have had a number of visitations or sightings of Count Saint-Germain after his supposed death. On the eve of the French Revolution he appeared with a drastic warning as to the fate of Queen and country. 'You are a terrible prophet!', exclaimed the Countess, 'When shall I see you again?' The answer came: 'Five times more; do not wish for the sixth'. In 1821, the year before she died, the Countess pinned a note to her original manuscript which read:

I saw M. de St. Germain again, and always to my unspeakable surprise: at the assassination of the Queen; at the coming of the 18th Brumaire; the day following the death of the Duc d'Enghien; in the month of January, 1813; and on the eve of the murder of the Duc de Berri. I await the sixth visit when God wills.

While these memoirs were published too late for Pushkin to have known them, it is clear that Saint-Germain already had a reputation, in certain circles at least, as an 'angel of death' and the 'midnight bridegroom'.

References and Sources for Note

Odoevsky, Vladimir, 'Letter IV [*to Countess Ye.P. Rostopchina*]', in *The Salamander and other Gothic Tales*, translated by Neil Cornwell (Bristol Classical Press: Bristol, 1992). Original first published 1839.

Encyclopedia Britannica, 11th edn (1911).

Oakley, I. Cooper, *The Comte de St. Germain: The Secret of Kings* (Samuel Weiser Inc.: New York, 1970). First published Milan, 1912.

Givry, Emile Grillot de, *Illustrated Anthology of Sorcery, Magic and Alchemy* (Zachary Kwintner Books Ltd: London, 1991). First published Paris, 1929.

Preedy, George R., *The Courtly Charlatan: The Enigmatic Comte de St. Germain* (Herbert Jenkins: London, 1942).

Wilson, Colin, *The Occult* (Mayflower: St Albans, 1973). First published London, 1971.

Eco, Umberto, *Foucault's Pendulum*, translated by William Weaver (QPD: London, 1990). First published 1989.

Postscript to the Appendix

1. A somewhat more scholarly biography, entitled *The Comte de Saint-Germain: Last Scion of the House of Rakoczy* (East-West Publications: London and The Hague, 1988), by Jean Overton Fuller, corrects or particularises many of the details outlined above. According to her version of events, Saint-Germain was the illegitimate son of Francis Rákóczy and Princess Violante of Bavaria (by marriage a Medici), born in 1694. She also, however, posits the theosophical theory that he, at the same time, as a 'Master Rákóczy', 'took over' the identity and memory of his father, the deposed Prince of Transylvania. Little else of Pushkinian interest emerges from her account, except that Saint-Germain may have sailed to the Battle of Chesmë in 1770, with Aleksei Orlov (under the name 'General Saltikov'), as a preliminary to a far-fetched scheme to reclaim Transylvania with Catherine the Great's support. Ms Fuller also doubts the authenticity of a number of Saint-Germainian sources, such as the memoirs of Countess Adhémar (1836) and Madame de Hausset (1824) – the latter of which Pushkin could have known. However, it is arguable that, for our purposes, the legends surrounding Saint-Germain remain more interesting than whatever may have been the truth.

2. Wolf Schmid (in his *Proza kak poeziia*, St Petersburg, 1998, 137-44) includes an appendix to his overall essay which he entitles 'Saint-Germain, Casanova, Tomsky, Pushkin – mages of storytelling'. An extended German version is to be found in *Die Welt der Slaven* (43, 1998, 153-60). Drawing in the main on sources in German, he links Swedenborg to the Pushkinian Saint-Germain, and to Hermann (affirming that, for instance, 'the historical Saint-Germain continued the crystallographic researches of Swedenborg': 139), and stresses Casanova's acclamation of Saint-Germain's phenomenal prowess as a raconteur. This last point leads him to nominate Saint-Germain the (dubious) anecdotist as prime mover in a chain of (tall) storytelling, continued by Tomsky and Pushkin himself, that has astonished first Hermann and subsequently countless readers – and continues to this day to engage literary critics and historians.

3. Chelsea Quinn Yarbro's novel *Hôtel Transylvania* (New English Library: London, 1981; first published in 1978) is the first in a sequence of novels featuring Saint-Germain (also known here as, among other things, 'Prinz Ragoczy of Transylvania') as a timeless, but benevolent, vampire (according to Casanova, at society dinners his eloquence always sparkled but he never ate; see Schmid, 1998: 142-3). Establishing, as it were, Saint-Germain's credentials, *Hôtel Transylvania* is set within its protagonist's known historical lifetime – namely in and around the Paris of 1743. Portrayed as a kind of immortal knight-errant, Saint-Germain rescues the heroine Madeleine from extreme forms of Satanic abuse and sacrifice, whilst apparently claiming her, at her own urging, for the vampiric cause. Alchemical expertise, advice on gambling (in a possible nod towards Pushkin), the lack of a reflection, and mind-reading abilities are to be numbered among his qualities. A combination of the vampiric horror story and the mildly pornographic bodice-ripper, *Hôtel Transylvania* is followed by a number of relatively autonomous novels, setting Saint-Germain in a variety of historical epochs and far-flung realms. For a summary of Yarbro's *oeuvre*, see John Clute and John Grant, *The Encyclopedia of Fantasy* (Orbit: London, 1997, 1041-2).

Index